CONTENTS

Author: **Denis McCarthy**

Researcher: **David Benton**

D0167603

BAILE ÁTHA CLIATH
ARNA FHOILSIÚ AG **OIFIG AN tSOLÁTHAIR**

Le ceannach díreach ón
OIFIG DHÍOLTA FOILSEACHÁN RIALTAIS,
TEACH SUN ALLIANCE, SRÁID THEACH LAIGHEAN, BAILE ÁTHA CLIATH 2
nó tríd an bpost ó
FOILSEACHÁIN RIALTAIS, AN RANNÓG POST-TRÁCHTA
51 FAICHE STIABHNA, BAILE ÁTHA CLIATH 2
(Teil: 01-6476834/35/36/37, Fax: 01-647 6843)
nó trí aon díoltóir leabhar.

DUBLIN
PUBLISHED BY THE **STATIONERY OFFICE**

To be purchased from the
GOVERNMENT PUBLICATIONS SALES OFFICE,
SUN ALLIANCE HOUSE, MOLESWORTH STREET, DUBLIN 2
or by mail order from
GOVERNMENT PUBLICATIONS, POSTAL TRADE SECTION,
51 ST. STEPHEN'S GREEN, DUBLIN 2
(Tel: 01-6476834/35/36/37, Fax: 01-647 6843)
or through any bookseller

Design : **Niamh Lehane**

Right *Selection of finds from Dublin Castle*
archaeological excavations:- knife handle
13th century, and dice, bone pins (or
bodkins) and comb 10th - 12th centuries.

Introduction

Dublin Castle is at the historic core of Dublin. In fact, the city gets its name from the Black Pool harbour, or Dubhlinn, which occupied the site of the present Castle Gardens.

It is most likely that a Gaelic ring fort existed on the adjacent Hazel Wood Ridge, on the site of the Upper Castle Yard. This strategically important and easily defended location, at the junction of the Liffey and Poddle Rivers, guarded the harbour and the four long-distance roadways that converged nearby.

This was also a significant place during Viking times and part of the town's tenth century defensive bank is on view beneath the floor level of the Powder Tower.

The Upper Castle Yard today corresponds closely with the almost rectangular castle established by King John in 1204 AD, which became an indispensable feature of the town's defenses and the most important fortification in Ireland.

The Castle remained in continuous occupation and was adapted to suit changing requirements – in particular following the great fire of 1684 when it became a palace rather than a fortress. Although much of the present architecture dates from the eighteenth century, sections of the original moat, curtain wall and town wall, as well as the Record Tower and the bases of the other massive corner towers are still visible.

Dublin Castle functioned as the seat of English colonial rule and the centre of military, political and social affairs. At various times it housed the Chief Governors of Ireland, Police Headquarters, State Prison, Treasury, Royal Mint, Armory, War Office, Privy Council, Courts of Justice and the Parliament.

In 1922, it was the location of the handover to the new Irish State. Since independence, it has transformed into a place of national prestige.

NOTE TO THE READER

If you wish to bypass background information, begin with the essential history of the establishment of the Castle on page 16.

The Castle's Visitor Attractions feature from page 128.

⟨D⟩ubhlinn : Gaelic Dublin

The murals of Irish mythology in the Érin Room of Dublin Castle's State Apartments depict the five ancient legendary invasions of Ireland – in accordance with the eighth-century *Lebor Gabála*, or *Book of Invasions*. The Partholonians came from Macedonia via Iberia and settled in the plain of Moynalty, Co. Dublin. They were almost totally annihilated by plague 600 years later and were buried at Tallaght, Co. Dublin (from the Gaelic *tamhlacht* – meaning plague burial place). The next invaders were the Nemedians who originated in Scythia, present day Ukraine

below Amergin calming the storm: Érin Room mural by Tom Curtin.

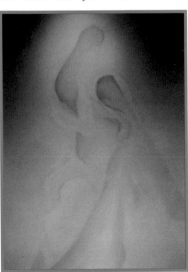

and came in thirty-four ships. Following their overwhelming defeat by the piratical Formorians, the survivors emigrated to Scotland. Great Britain is said to be named after one of their chieftains – Britán Mael.[1]

The third group of settlers was the pastoral Fir Bolgs – an offshoot of the Celtic Belgae tribe that inhabited parts of northwest France and Belgium. They worshipped Bolga – the god of lightning, and their men (or *fir* in Gaelic) were famed for their equestrian skills. The spectacular stone fort of Dún Aengus, perched on the Atlantic precipice, is reputed to have been one of their last strongholds – following their defeats at the two battles of Moytirra, Co. Sligo.

The second panel features Érin, Banba and Fódhla, the queens or goddesses of the mystical *Tuatha Dé Danann* – the People of the goddess Dana – a conquering Celtic people from the River Elbe area of Germany. Following defeat by the Milesians, they were said to have entered the otherworld realm to live in the cairns and burial mounds dispersed throughout the Irish landscape and formed the nucleus for the fairies and leprechauns of later popular Irish folklore. Érin remains the Gaelic name for Ireland.

The third mural (see opposite page) depicts Amhairghin Glungheal, the supreme Druid of the Celtic Milesians (followers of Míl) who came from Galicia, Spain, in 331 BC, and were the last of the early invaders. Here he is shown calming the storm that had caused his wife to drown, and so enabled the invasion fleet to land in Kenmare Bay. He is known as the 'Father of Irish poetry' on account of his 'Song of Amhairghin'. In this he invoked the land of Ireland:

I SPEAK FOR ÉRIN

SAILED AND FERTILE SEA

FERTILE FRUITFUL MOUNTAINS

FRUITFUL MOIST WOODS.[2]

He saw himself as being powerfully in tune with the energy of nature:

I AM THE BREAKER THREATENING DOOM.

I AM A TIDE THAT DRAGS TO DEATH.

I AM A TEAR THE SUN LETS FALL.[3]

Ireland was actually first peopled in the Mesolithic, or Middle Stone, Age c.8000 BC, with the coming of semi-nomadic hunter-gatherers. This had become possible following the ending of the last Ice Age, the warming of the climate and the retreat of the glaciers which had buried all but the extreme south of the country. They lived in an environment of extensive forests, rivers and lakes, kept dogs, possessed flint weapons and ate wild boar, hares, birds, fish, apples and nuts. Population numbers were small and over the following 2,000 years, may have risen to 3,000. The remains of a midden (rubbish heap) on Dalkey Island, Co. Dublin, has been dated at c.5000 BC.

Neolithic or New Stone Age farmers arrived c.4000 BC, during the warmest epoch of post-glacial times. Due to the dangers of shipping cattle, it is likely that they came the shortest sea routes from Britain, but they had international trading links and probably were part of the much larger migration that originated in southeast Europe and spread out through central and western Europe. They built the Boyne Valley megalithic passage graves in Co. Meath c.3200 BC (a UNESCO world heritage site) where they had felled the dense woods with wooden handled, polished stone (porcellanite) axes – some of which were quarried at Feltrim Hill, north Co. Dublin and have been found nearby at Sutton (on the opposite end of Dublin Bay to Dalkey). They also grew wheat and barley on land tilled by wooded ploughs with stone blades.

At a time of significant population shift in continental Europe, c.2000 BC, two groups of new settlers imported the horse, 'beaker pottery', metalworking, and the Bronze Age into Ireland. Evidence of their cultures survives in their burial cists in the Phoenix Park (2 km west of the Castle), the hill top cairns on the Dublin Mountains and their renowned gold ornamental treasures, which can be seen in the National Museum, Kildare Street.

The Celts brought the Iron Age around 700 BC – during a colder, wetter era that coincided with a period of growth of peat deposits, increased agricultural activity and prosperity. The Greeks and Romans knew them as *Keltoi* – barbarian tribes that lived to their north and were independent and unrelated except through language. On account of population pressures, they extended their territories to include France (Gaul), Iberia and Britain and may have reached Ireland in two waves from Galicia and Britain. In view of the considerable coastal movement of people in the Bay area – the present Dublin Castle site may have been occupied by human settlement at this time (if not earlier).

These Celtic colonizers and the probable succeeding waves of settlers of the sixth and fourth centuries BC are most unlikely to have amounted to large-scale population immigration, because of the immense practical difficulties involved in voyaging to the island of Ireland. However, renowned for their well-organised and sophisticated tribal society, their superior iron weaponry and 'warlike fearlessness', it is possible and perhaps probable that their warrior class gained control.

Over time they would have intermarried and assimilated with the native Irish, so forming the Gaels – an ethnic term for the population of Ireland, which was employed by the Irish themselves at least by the eighth century AD. [4] The resultant rich Gaelic culture and language, with its elaborate system of law and custom, were to predominate until modern times.

Dublin originated in the area in and around the present Dublin Castle site, on the southern bank of the estuary of the River Liffey where it entered Dublin Bay. In the Iron Age, the lower reaches of the Liffey were much shallower and are estimated to have been at least four times wider than at present (see map opposite), with the mouth slightly east of Grattan (Capel Street) Bridge. It was known in Irish as *An Ruirthech* – the raging or tempestuous one, owing to its tendency to flash flood. In 770 AD it justified its name when a raiding party from the Kingdom of Ulster was drowned as it returned victoriously from a battle at Áth Cliath.

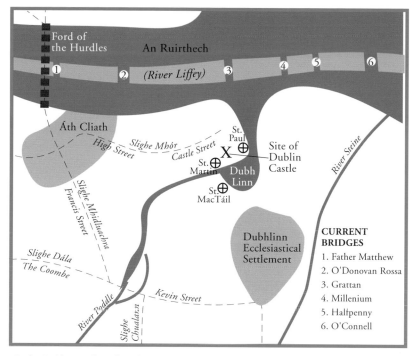

Gaelic Dublin, with modern features superimposed.

Áth Cliath, the 'Ford of the Hurdles', situated just upriver from the Four Courts, was a major Liffey crossing of perhaps 300m width. It was constructed of interwoven wattles which were anchored by posts and rocks to the gravel riverbed and allowed people and animals to cross the mud flats at low tide. Áth Cliath was also the name of the adjacent fishing and farming settlement and is today the Gaelic name for Dublin.

In the area occupied by the present Dublin Castle Gardens, there was a sheltered deep dark pool or harbour, known as the Dubhlinn – black pool in Gaelic – from which Dublin gets its name. (Here, archaeological excavations on the Chester Beatty Library site uncovered a quarry that had been back filled with silt.) The harbour, or pool, formed where the now-underground River Poddle joined the Liffey. It is likely to have been flooded at high tide and was the staging post for exports and imports for the village-type Dubhlinn ecclesiastical settlement that lay directly to the south of the present Castle Gardens. Its oval shape can be traced in the street pattern of Peter Row, Upper and Lower

Stephen Street and Johnson Place. (Many Christian communities existed in Ireland even before St. Patrick's mission, *c* 432-461 AD, and the process of outright conversion of the Irish was completed long after his death).

The Churches of St. Paul and St. Martin were destroyed during the construction of medieval Dublin Castle. The Church of St. Michael le Pole was situated immediately southwest of the present Castle, outside the medieval town walls, between Great Ship Street and Chancery Lane. Originally dedicated to St. MacTáil, its later name of 'le Pole' refers to the pool harbour. It featured the only round tower in Dublin, which was partly demolished after being hit by a lightning bolt in 1775 and is included in one of Waldré's canvas ceiling paintings in St. Patrick's Hall, State Apartments (see p.14).

The site of the Upper Castle Yard was at the eastern end of the *Druim Choll Coill* – The Hazel Wood Ridge. It overlooked the Poddle and the Liffey and was above the flood plains of both. Most probably, a Gaelic ring fort or *rath* existed here to guard the harbour, the Áth Cliath river crossing and the four major long-distance roadways that converged nearby at the junction of Francis Street and Cornmarket (outside medieval New Gate – see image p.35). Significantly, *Slighe Mhór*, the road from the west, terminated at the High Cross near the site of Dublin Castle.[5]

below St. Patrick lighting the Pascal fire on the Hill of Slane, by Vincenzo Waldré, c 1794: St. Patrick's Hall, State Apartments (See also photo on p.137)

Dyflinn : Viking Dublin

Ireland remained free from foreign invasion for more than 1,000 years – until the summer of 795 AD, when Norwegian Vikings made a 'hit and run' attack on the monastery of Lambay Island, immediately north of Dublin Bay. As was the case throughout much of Europe, this set the pattern for such raids on rich targets for the next three decades.

These were the greatest seafarers and most feared raiders of their age. A verse from the margins of a ninth-century Irish monastic manuscript shows the terror they provoked, forcing many monks to flee to mainland Europe:

BITTER IS THE WIND TONIGHT
IT TOSSES THE OCEAN'S WHITE HAIR.
TONIGHT I FEAR NOT THE FIERCE
WARRIORS OF NORWAY
COURSING THE IRISH SEA.[6]

In 837 AD, according to the Annals of Ulster, a fleet of sixty-five 'Dragon' warships appeared at the mouth of the Liffey and, five years later, a force under the command of King Ivar Turgesius, 'Servant of Thor', captured the harbour of Dublin. They then 'threw up a fort on the high ridge where Dublin Castle later arose.'[7]

While this last assertion is speculative (as no archaeological evidence has yet been found) the site was clearly ideal for their fortress, with the River Poddle forming a natural defensive boundary on two sides and supplying drinking water – factors that would have been of primary importance in their choice of location. In addition, the adjacent Dubhlinn harbour provided the near perfect position for their *longphort* or ship harbour by giving shelter from and ease of access to the Irish Sea.

This became their pirate lair from where they raided and plundered, but an alliance of Leinstermen drove them out in 902 AD and burnt down the fortress. However, they returned seventeen years later, in greater numbers, with Danish colleagues and with greater purpose. They settled on the still evident ridge between the Castle and Christ Church Cathedral and developed a lucrative trade in silver and slaves. They fortified this proto town or pre-urban nucleus of Dyflinn (corruption of Dubhlinn) with encircling earthen banks topped with strong wooden palisade fencing. Part of one of the earliest town defences is on view in the Undercroft in Dublin Castle, where the tenth-century stone-faced revetment offered protection against erosion by the Poddle. [8]

The name *Dún Dyflinn* (*dún* is the Gaelic word for fort or fortress) came into usage shortly afterwards and so, it appears that a Viking fortress may again have occupied the Castle site and became the focal point of the town's growth and development. Excavations on the riverward side of the Castle (in Temple Bar West) located the remains of a succession of ninth-century Viking sunken houses and most archaeologists agree that the settlement plots developed around the fortress.

Over the following 250 years, Dyflinn evolved into an important, wealthy trading and manufacturing centre and became capital of the territory of Dyflinnarskiri – from Skerries to Arklow and east to Leixlip. It was also the largest Viking town in the North Atlantic, being strategically important in their interconnecting Russian, Mediterranean and Arctic trade routes and was recommended to young voyagers in the Norse Sagas.

This urban development took place despite some major setbacks, including the Battle of Áth Cliath in 947 AD, when the troops of the High King, Congalach Cnogba, overcame the town's defenders and laid siege to the *Dún*. Another High King, Máel Sechnaill II, captured

the town in 990 AD and, nine years later, his army combined with that of Brian Boru, King of Munster, and burned the 'Dún and Dyflinn's houses, divisions, ships and all other structures.'

From this time of rebuilding, it became a mixed Irish (Hiberno) and Norse town, where intermarriage was common; the population may have reached 5,000 and life expectancy was 35 years. The *Dún* of *Dyflinn* was described in the *Book of Leinster* (*c*.1160) as being one of the 'Seven Wonders of Ireland'.

The Vikings began to convert to Christianity but gave allegiance to Canterbury, rather than to the Irish

ecclesiastical capital of Armagh. This was to bring severe consequences some decades later.

At the battle of Clontarf in 1014 – which took place a few kilometres north-east of the Castle and east of the River Tolka – an army under Brian Boru decisively defeated the Dublin and Orkney Vikings and their Leinster allies, led by King Máel Morda. It was believed that the raising of the cursed black Raven Banner to the God Odin led to certain victory. However, as it also guaranteed the death of the standard bearer, no one was found to carry it on that Good Friday. The bloody 'hand to hand' struggle between the tightly packed armies

above Sculpture of King Brian Boru, at the entrance to the Crypt of the Chapel Royal.

raged 'from high tide to high tide'. Eventually, following the crushing of their centre shield wall, several thousand of the 'foreigners' were killed or drowned in the resultant rout.

Boru was killed by Brodar – the champion warrior who had commanded one phalanx, wore his hair tucked under his belt and remained dedicated to the 'old ways and Gods'. His successors failed to accomplish his dream of uniting all Ireland. The Vikings paid tribute to the Irish, their ability to further expand arrested and King Sitric III ('Silkenbeard') continued to reign as King of Dyflinn (989-1038, and the Vikings of Ireland and England). They were still there more than a 100 years later when the Normans arrived at their gates.

left Viking Dublin c.940AD, looking southwards with the Dublin/Wicklow mountains in the background and the River Liffey in the foreground, by Stephen Conlin.

Divelin : Norman Dublin & Establishment of the Castle

The Normans were 'grandchildren' of the Vikings who had settled in Normandy, northwest France, and had conquered England in 1066. Ireland was to suffer a similar fate a century later.

Dermot MacMurrough, King of Leinster, was deposed in 1166 by the new High King, Rory O'Connor, following his failed attempt to attain that post. The Dublin Vikings co-operated with his expulsion because of his 'violent, overbearing and ferocious' temperament and Dermot fled to seek help from King Henry II (with whom he had family connections) at his court in Aquitaine. There he received royal protection and authorisation to recruit Flemish and Welsh Anglo-Norman mercenaries.

This was perfect timing for Henry and presented him with the ideal opportunity, as proposals for a conquest of Ireland had been explored at the English Royal Council, at Winchester, in 1155. Nicholas Breakspear, son of a Cistercian monk, had become Pope Adrian IV – the only Englishman ever to occupy that office – and Henry sought approval from him

to conduct a conquering crusade of Ireland. That same year, Pope Adrian issued 'The Bull Laudabiliter' – a papal epistle in which he delivered his authorisation: 'We, seconding your pious and commendable intention with the favour it deserves and granting a benign assent to your petition, are well pleased that for the enlargement of the bounds of the church, for the restraint of vice, the correction of evil manners, the culture of all virtues and the advancement of the Christian religion, you should enter into that island and effect what will conduce to the salvation thereof and to the honour of God.'

The Anglo-Norman invasion fleet of 'grey foreigners' landed at Baginbun, Co. Wexford, on 1st May 1169. The Irish – lightly clad and armed only with battleaxes, slings and short swords – couldn't match the close order charge of the technologically advanced, chain mail clad heavy cavalry, assisted by infantry and long and crossbow archers: 'At Baginbun, Ireland was lost and won.' Neither could the Viking towns of Wexford and Waterford, which fell within three months of each other.

In September of the following

left King John of England, by Du Noyer.   *right* Justiciar de Londres, by Du Noyer.

year, 5,000 Anglo-Normans force-marched through the 'impenetrable' Wicklow Mountains and so bypassed O'Connor's much larger army. On the 21st they attacked the eastern Dame Gate (at current Dame Street junction close to the Castle's Palace Street Gate). A second attack by shock troops at the western – Christ Church – end of town proved decisive: 'The Vikings were slaughtered in their citadel.'

Asculf MacThorkil (the recently deposed twenty-fifth Viking King of Dublin) led one of a number of serious attempts to re-take the town in 1171. His troops, clad in chain mail, with conical helmets and two-handed battleaxes, landed at the strand beside the Steyne. (The now underground river illustrated on p.7 took its name from this Viking longstone possession marker, which stood at the current junction of Townsend and Hawkins Streets.) 'Fired by revenge' and led by their champion berserker, John the Wode, they launched an attack on Dame Gate, but were routed in a pincer movement involving a cavalry unit breakout from Pole Gate. Asculf was taken prisoner to the Norman headquarters at the 'Castle of Divelin' (probably on the southeastern part of the present Upper Castle Yard). Defiant to the end, he was beheaded on the orders of Miles de Cogan, Commander of the 'Castle and Donjon'. Thus finally ending the almost 300-year Viking reign of Dublin.

A few months later, King Henry arrived in order to keep his adventurers in check and to ensure

14

that the new resilient colony would remain under his control. He received the submission of most of the Irish Chieftains, who thought it wise to capitulate, perhaps in the mistaken belief that Henry would control his battle-hardened knights and mercenaries. One of the St. Patrick's Hall paintings commemorates the event.

The Irish Bishops also swore allegiance to him, on the presumption that it would heal the rift with Canterbury and that benefits would accrue to the people – including their desired repression of the Irish laws and customs that permitted promiscuity, polygamy and divorce. Pope Adrian wrote to them: 'We have further learnt from your letters that our dearest son in

Christ, Henry noble King of the English, prompted by God, has, with his assembled forces, subjected to his rule that barbarous and uncivilised people, ignorant of divine law, and that what was unlawfully being practiced in your country is already with God's help, beginning to decrease, and we are overjoyed.' [9]

Henry stayed for three months and issued a charter, (which is now kept in the Dublin Archives): 'Know ye that I have given and granted and by the present charter confirmed to my men of Bristol my city of Dublin to dwell in.' He made Hugh de Lacy his Bailiff – in effect the first Justiciar. (The latter title of the Chief Governor or Viceroy of Ireland [meaning in

above *King Henry 11 receiving the submission of Irish chieftains in 1171 AD, by Waldré. (The Round Tower of the church of St. MacTáil had collapsed before this painting was commissioned)*

place of, or second to the King] was later to change to Lord Deputy, and later still to Lord Lieutenant.) The issuing of a second Royal charter granted his Dublin burgesses 'freedom from toll, passage, portage, lestage, pavage, murage, quayage, carriage and all custom' duties and ensured the economic development of the town – the population of which increased to perhaps 10,000.

The Hiberno-Norse (Vikings) were tolerated at first but further waves of settlers forced them out and across the Liffey, where they established the new suburb of Ostmanstown, meaning town of men of the east and now called Oxmantown, in the open commonage of the same name. Over time, they were assimilated into the Irish population.

The Anglo-Normans chose to site their citadel in the southeast angle of the Viking town, for the very same strategic reasons as those of the Vikings and Gaelic Irish – it being on the eastern edge of an easily defended ridge, at the confluence of two rivers, with easy access to Dubhlinn harbour and Dublin Bay. It is assumed that their first fortification or 'campaign castle', which housed the knights stationed by King Henry, was that of the motte and bailey type – a typical defence feature in newly acquired territory, which had been developed to its greatest effect during the process of conquest. This consisted of an enclosure (bailey) from which the earth had been piled into a huge, very steep-sided, mound topped with a tower (motte) and fenced at the summit and the base. The bailey was connected to the motte by a bridge and a ditch surrounded the whole figure of eight complex. Stone could replace the wooden features and tower as military conditions allowed.

A number of historical references indicate that an early Norman castle or tower occupied part of the present Dublin Castle site. Strongbow (Richard Fitzgilbert, alias de Clare), who died in 1176, succeeded MacMurrough as Lord of Leinster and received property adjoining the Castle walls.[10] Justiciar Peter Pipard, chief governor and principal law officer, tried a case in the Castle in 1192, in which the plaintiff, William Le Brun, was successful and the accused was 'bound to the peace'. However, following the second sitting, Le Brun was attacked and killed on the drawbridge and his body thrown into the north moat. Nothing of that early castle survived the subsequent extensive building works, other than part of an enclosing curtain stonewall which was uncovered in archaeological excavations beside the present Bermingham Tower.

'Evil' Prince John was King Henry 11's rebellious fourth son (and the younger brother of Richard 'the Lionheart'). Henry – the most effective of all Britain's monarchs – appointed him Lord of Ireland and sent him to rule with the support of experienced administrators in 1185. But John was extremely unpopular, alienated both colonists and Irish and returned home within six months. Later he too became King but his oppressive government, treachery and unbridled self interest resulted in the loss of Anjou and Normandy (and in the rebellion in 1215 that produced the English charter of liberties: Magna Carta), following which he took the opportunity to further secure his lordship in Ireland.

On the 30th August 1204, King John issued the following mandate to his 'trusty and well beloved' cousin, Justiciar Meiler FitzHenry (1199-1208): 'You have given us to understand that you have no safe place for the custody of our treasure, and because for this reason and for many others, we are in need of a strong fortress in Dublin. We command you to erect a castle there, in such a competent place as you may consider to be suitable if need be for the defence of the city as well to curb it, if occasion shall so require, making it as strong as you can with good fosses [ditches or moat] and strong walls. But you are first to build one tower, to which a castle and palace and other requirements may be conveniently added: for all of these you have our authority.'

Works were begun on a much larger site than the earlier castle. Progress was slow at first, but the visit of John in 1210, with master craftsmen expert in military fortifications, injected more urgency and purpose and provided upgraded design. He also established an exchequer to manage Royal Revenues and strengthened his control of the Barons. Four years later, he funded improvement works to the old town walls, which may have proceeded at the same time as the Castle's curtain walls.[11]

Henry de Londres, Archbishop of Dublin and Justiciar (1213-15

and 1221-24, see image p.13), is credited with primary responsibility for construction of the new Castle. Many buildings were removed to make way for the new works including some belonging to the Priory and convent of the Holy Trinity (Christ Church) – for which they were compensated, and the churches of St. Paul (near the present Chapel Royal) and St. Martin (near Ship Street) – for which de Londres remunerated himself. His double appointment appears to have been a crafty manoeuvre by the King to facilitate the unopposed removal of these churches – which, interestingly, had survived the Viking occupation.

Mighty Dublin Castle, with extensive encircling moat, was completed by 1230. A twin-towered

town gateway, with drawbridge and portcullis, stood at the centre of the north curtain (perimeter) wall, with a corresponding smaller D-shaped, middle tower in the south and formidable circular, projecting, towers at each corner. These defences were so strong that no keep (central tower) was necessary. The almost rectangular enclosure of $1/2$ hectare ($1 1/4$ acres) was mainly occupied by domestic and military buildings and included bakery, kitchen, workshop, chapel and prison. The Castle, or King's Hall, 'after the manner of the Hall of Canterbury', was the centre of activities and served as Court House and Parliament.

Nevertheless, the townspeople were always vulnerable to attacks by the Irish Clansmen. On Easter Monday 1209, a party of 500 Bristol merchants and their families were slaughtered by the O'Byrnes and the O'Tooles of Wicklow, while picnicking in the groves of Cullenwood, now in the suburb of Ranelagh, 5 kilometres south-east of the Castle. This 'Black Monday' massacre was commemorated annually until 1690.

A Royal charter of 1221 enabled the citizens to further strengthen the town walls by levying tolls on

left Norman Dublin c.1275, by Stephen Conlin. (Note dominant position of the Castle and see Viking Dublin on P.11)

goods brought in for sale and gates were added or improved. A town-wide building programme was set in motion, which continued throughout the century. Suburbs grew outside the walls, especially around the powerful monastic houses and oak-framed houses, with clay or stone floors, became popular. The marshlands north of the original Viking town wall (at Cook Street/Essex Street) were reclaimed by the dumping of refuse, consolidated and secured by a succession of banks and revetments[12] (see illustration p.35). This resulted in a narrowing of the Liffey channel with greater depth of water for larger ships and substantially increased volumes of trade. Wooden and stone waterfronts were then completed at Merchants' and Wood Quays and defensive walls and towers added.

Justiciar Maurice Fitzgerald commanded the City Sheriff to design and implement a public-water delivery system in 1244, which would be paid for and maintained by the townspeople, water mill owners and town officials. All opposition was quashed. More than one third of the River Poddle's flow was diverted to a town cistern in James's Street and carried onwards in open elmwood conduits through the town to the Castle. (In time, these were supplemented and replaced with Dodder water and iron piping.)

Following the standardisation of weights and measures in 1244, the King's appointed Keeper in Ireland, Edward Biroun, was found guilty of interfering with same for his own gain and was delivered to Henry le Waleys, the Castle Constable (a post created on foot of a Royal mandate of 1220) and the Chief Jailer, Thomas Big. However, he escaped and was declared an outlaw. Successfull getaways, especially by rich prisoners, were regular occurrences but failures were far more common. Walter MacThorkil and three others were caught during one such attempt. They were hanged and his wife was imprisoned for supplying the coverlets with which they had made their escape ladder.

Stephen de Fulbourn, Bishop of Waterford and later Archbishop of Tuam, was Justiciar on three occasions between 1277-86. He imposed a large fine of £100 on Constable Philip Keling for releasing a Fr. O'Farrell who was under accusation of spying, but later found himself under investigation for 'irregularities' and was accused of misappropriating materials for his own use – including marble pillars from the Great Hall of the Castle which had been conveyed to his property at Dunbro, north Co. Dublin. Furthermore, he was found to have destroyed many of his records and to owe £13,235 to the Crown.

King Edward 1 issued a severe censure but allowed him to remain as Justiciar until his death, in consideration of 'his immense outlay on the fortifications of the King's castles in Ireland, in quelling wars and other matters' – namely, the substantial monies he had diverted to the Crown's coffers. The Treasurer, Nicholas de Clare, who had assembled the evidence against de Fulbourn, was imprisoned in the Castle for arrears on his account, although confiscation of goods and property was more usual in such cases. [13]

The years of colonial expansion and prosperity came to an end as the overall circumstances deteriorated. Internal quarrelling and disputes erupted between some colonial lords and magnates, such as the hostilities between the Fitzgeralds and the de Burghs (Burkes) over land titles. A major part of Dublin town burned to the ground in 1283. The Castle treasury became depleted, and the Justiciar's running expenses were drastically reduced, as exploitative policies and demands were made of him by the King, to finance military campaigns in Wales and especially in Scotland.

Neglect and near bankruptcy of the colonial administration prompted an Irish cultural and military resurgence and attacks became commonplace throughout this and the following century.

On 25th May 1315, Edward Bruce (a descendant of Dermot MacMurrough through the female line) landed at Larne, Co. Antrim, with 6,000 experienced soldiers fresh from their victory over the English at Bannockburn. His objective was the creation of a pan-Celtic alliance (including Wales) against England – the common enemy. The campaign would also help the war plans of his older brother, King Robert of Scotland, by disrupting supplies from Ireland to the English forces on their border. It did avert an invasion of western Scotland by a fleet of sixty ships, which Justiciar Rodger de Mortimer was ordered to provide two years later. Edward Bruce was crowned King of Ireland and was joined by many Ulster Chieftains and some Old English 'renegades'.

That autumn, a group of military specialists were sent to the Castle to assist Constable Henry de Badewe in his preparations for siege and the Dubliners in fortifying the town. The Mayor and bailiffs were ordered to provide the Castle with 1,000 crossbow arrows, coal, wheat, salt and grease, lead for the towers and internal buildings and a ship for transportation of stones. Production of crossbows was intensified in the Castle armoury, as regular manufacture of items such as nails, horseshoes, spades, catapults and siege engines was suspended. Those crucial to the exchequer, the Royal treasury and defence of the Castle were ordered to live within its walls, to ensure their safety against possible assassination by rebel sympathisers in the town.

The nearby bell tower of St. Marie del Dam was demolished, as it could provide a strategic vantage point for attackers, and the stone was used in necessary repairs to the Castle. (The tower of St. Werburg's Church received the same treatment, for similar reasons, in the nineteenth century.) Other materials were used for barricades and to extend the town's defensive wall along the new quays. A long wide ditch at right angles to the Liffey, which appears to have been a defensive feature dating from that time, was unearthed in archaeological excavations in Castle Street.

The Bishop of Down took refuge in the Castle in November 'where hostages had recently been received' to guarantee the loyalty of a number of Irish leaders. The following February, seven companions of the loyal Earl of Ulster, father-in-law of Robert Bruce, were killed during his forcible removal from St. Mary's Abbey by citizens led by the mayor. He was imprisoned in the Castle for six months.

Bruce's army defeated that of the Justiciar at Trim (Co. Meath) and again, against expectations, at the Battle of Ardscull (Co. Kildare) on 26th January 1316. His presence also encouraged the rebellion of many Clans in Munster and Leinster and the colony, attacked from all sides, was in grave peril.

Nonetheless, Justiciar Roger de Mortimer also had victories and

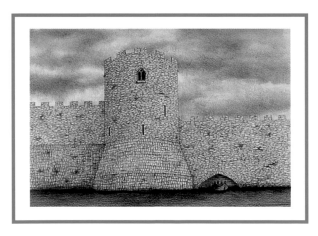

above Curtain wall, Powder Tower and boat in the River Poddle – having left the Castle moat via town wall archway, by Aisling Adams

overturned the early successes of the O'Tooles and O'Byrnes, (which included the massacre of the garrison of Castlekevin and the sacking of Rathcoole and Saggart, south-west Co. Dublin) and had 'four score of their heads set upon Dublin Castle'. He also imprisoned the survivors of Bruce's Isle of Man garrison there, along with the remnants of Scottish and Irish privateers who were defeated in the Irish Sea battle of May 1317.

Bruce's army twice came very near to Dublin town, from where their campfires in the present-day suburb of Castleknock could be seen. It was in extreme danger of being overrun and under severe pressure to surrender. The panic-stricken townspeople adapted a scorched-earth policy and burnt the Liffey Bridge and the western walled suburbs and farm lands. This denied food to Bruce's army, during the (European-wide) famine of 1315-18, which the rival armies had further aggravated, as according to *The Annals of Connaught*: 'they left neither wood nor meadow, neither corn nor crops, nor farmstead nor barn nor church, but they burnt them all.'

Faced with these defensive measures, lacking a siege train and with his army's resistance to disease weakened through hunger, Bruce's army retreated and Dublin was saved. On the 14th October 1318, with troop reinforcements from England, the new Justiciar Edmund Butler conclusively defeated Bruce's army at the Battle of Fochart (Co. Louth).

In 1328, two men were imprisoned in the Castle on charges of heresy. Adam Duff O'Toole was condemned for refuting the divinity of Jesus Christ and burnt at the stake at Hogges (now College) Green. Arnold le Poer, the Seneschal (feudal administrator) of Kilkenny, was jailed following his excommunication by Richard Ledrede, Bishop of Ossory, whom he described as a 'vagabond from England'. He had protected Alice Kyteler, who was under accusation of sorcery by the family of one of her four husbands, and consequentially became involved in a dispute with the Bishop who was interested in such matters to the point of obsession. He died in custody the following year.

The overall numbers of troops assigned to the Castle related directly to the perceived military and political climate of the time. The Justiciar's normal compliment of twenty mounted troops accompanied him on expeditions and regular tours of the country and some Anglo-Irish magnates provided the Castle with knights and horses as part of their feudal dues. Justiciar John Charlton brought 200 Welsh archers on his appointment in 1337 (during a period of upheaval) and six years later, Justiciar Ralph d'Ufford retained forty men at arms and 200 archers.

The most deadly enemy visited Dublin in 1348, when bubonic plague (known as the 'Black Death') arrived through the fishing village of Howth and further quickened the decline of the colony. It was carried by the black rat and spread to humans by fleas, which were plentiful (despite the widespread use of personal, sticky flea traps). The walled town was very small by modern standards; covering only 18 hectares (45 acres) and a citizen could walk from one side to the other in less than ten minutes. The plague thrived in these confined, congested conditions and in the even more crowded cells of the Castle. Some contemporary writers hailed it as 'the end of the world'. It is likely that almost half the townspeople died and the population declined to 6,000. Carts brought the bodies at night to be buried outside the walls at Black Pitts and New Street.[14] (The latter was so named in 1218 and still holds that name almost 800 years later.)

The power of the Dublin-based government was seriously weakened by the significantly high death rate among civil servants and administrators attached to the Castle and the overall mortality rate had a particularly destructive effect on this small corner of empire, where population numbers had always been of prime importance for survival. The plague left a base of infection which was to surface repeatedly for decades to come.[15]

From this time, the decline of the colony accelerated. King Edward III, fearing that it would totally fail, appointed his third son as Justiciar 1361-66. In advance of his arrival, Lionel of Clarence commanded the refurbishment of his accommodation in the Castle to a standard worthy of his princely status and pronounced that he was "wonderfully eager to wreak revenge" on the O'Mores of Laois, for their killing of Justiciar de Mortimer. He established a jousting ground, with wooden castle and paling, in the courtyard and had a barge built, possibly for use as a pleasure craft to carry members of the Court from the postern gate adjoining the Powder Tower to 'the Castle garden and arbours' (see image p.20). This garden, on part of the site of the former Dubhlinn or Pool of Dublin, was first documented almost fifty years previously (and was extensively enlarged and enhanced by Lord Deputy Wentworth in 1633). [16]

Lionel married Elizabeth Burke, heiress to the great Norman family's vast estates in Ulster and

Connaught. However, he was over ambitious in his introduction of the Statutes of Kilkenny (1366) which failed in their objectives of excluding the 'inferior, degenerate' native Irish from the colony and reversing the 'contamination' of Irish language, customs, dress and hairstyles which were being increasingly adopted. Furthermore, his military gains, won mainly in Leinster and Munster with a combined force of English and locally raised forces, were lost following his return to England. Building works and indeed routine maintenance works in the Castle appear to have ceased also as, fourteen years later, Justiciar Edmund Mortimer (son in law of Lionel) declared it to be an unfit location in which to hold meetings of the Council and Parliament.

In 1394, King Richard II came with a great army of 10,000 men in order to reverse the continued contraction of the colony. Presumably works were implemented in the Castle in advance. As a result of his military successes in Leinster and diplomatic missions throughout the country, almost all the Irish kings capitulated, including Donagh O'Byrne – ally of Art MacMurrough, King of Leinster – who submitted to him in the Castle on the following 19th February. MacMurrough, had not been deterred by the execution of several of his immediate predecessors by the forces of the Justiciar and was the main military target of the campaign.

Richard left in 1395 having failed to arbitrate successfully between the Irish chieftains and the magnates. Nor did his military intervention bring long-term recovery to the

above Art MacMurrough's troops confront Richard II's army in 1399.

colony, as his successes could only have been sustained by a continued effort for which the resources were not available.

King Richard landed at Waterford with a smaller second expedition in June 1399, which was harassed by 'hit and run' attacks by MacMurrough's troops and 'occupied Divelin' on the 1st July. A priest of the Chapel Royal had been dispatched in advance to inspect repairs to the Castle's accommodation, so it appears that it again became the Royal residence. During his stay, Richard was warned that his cousin Henry Bolingbroke, Duke of Lancaster, had returned to England from exile and mobilised support and so, he left hurriedly on the 27th. A stockpile of weapons for use by the infantry, bowmen and cavalry in the aborted offensive was abandoned in the Castle. This included two chests of bows, 31 pipes of arrows, 141 coats of mail and 335 large shields and lances. Sixteen cannons were returned to the Tower of London the following year.

This campaign cost the 32-year-old his crown and his life, as now his support dwindled and he suffered two military defeats within two weeks. William Shakespeare invoked strong sympathy for 'unkinged Richard' in the tragic finale of the play *Richard II*: 'Cry woe, destruction, ruin and decay. The worst is death and death will have his day'.

He was murdered in Pontefract Castle and Bolingbroke was crowned King Henry IV in Westminster Abbey. These events instigated the dynastic struggle that later exploded into the (English Civil) Wars of the Roses.

During the fifteenth century, England's main military campaigns were in France. The Hundred Years War restarted, but early conquests were ultimately lost, mainly due to the efforts of Joan of Arc (Jeanne d'Arc). Meanwhile, the Castle based Justiciars and Lord Deputies continued their planning, organising and funding of countless military expeditions, especially south of the 'Pale' – the English 'Land of Peace' – where, in 1467, the rebellious Old English Fitzgeralds (Earls of Kildare and Desmond) were the focus of the 'renowned legal authority' of Lord Deputy Tiptoft, former Treasurer of England.

Despite these considerable efforts, the Irish colony remained isolated, neglected and starved of resources and shrank even further. By 1515, the power of the Dublin government was effective only in a territory of less than 100km by 50km, (60 by 30 miles) of 'the four obedient counties of the Pale' – Dublin, Louth, Meath and Kildare.[17]

The Revolt of Silken Thomas

'Beyond the Pale', the great magnates exercised control over their own lordships, in large expanses of territory. It was then Royal policy to appoint the most powerful leader of the Fitzgerald or Butler Houses as Lord Deputy. The strongest at this time was Garret Mór Fitzgerald, Earl of Kildare, who held the post, not at Dublin Castle but at his stronghold of Maynooth Castle (until 1513, when he was shot dead in a skirmish with the O'Mores). His townhouse was in the suburbs at St. Thomas Court and a report of that time stated that Dublin Castle 'wherein the courts are kept is ruinous and likely to fall.'

During the Wars of the Roses (1455-87), the Fitzgeralds took an active part in plotting and promoting the ultimately failed attempts by the House of York to secure possession of the English Crown. The Yorkist allegiance of the majority of the Anglo-Irish colony originated in the period when Richard, Duke of York, served two terms as Lord Lieutenant. (One of his sons was born in the Castle in 1449 and another became King Edward 1V, 1461-83.) However, the Butlers of Ormond, Co. Kilkenny, supported the opposing House of Lancaster and

below St. Mary's Abbey, where Silken Thomas 'flung down his sword of office' in 1534.

continual rivalry between them and the Fitzgeralds led to repeated brawls in Dublin town.

Even Yorkist King Edward IV endeavoured to curb Garret's inordinate power by withdrawing the seal of office in 1478 and appointing Lord Henry Grey as Lord Deputy instead. However, the Castle Constable, Sir James Keating (presumably on Garret's orders) strengthened the garrison, destroyed the drawbridge and refused entry to Grey, who then summoned the Parliament in Trim, Co. Meath, in a further failed attempt to secure his appointment. King Richard III later reversed his brother's direction and restored Garret to the post. Keating was appointed Castle Constable for life.

Garret, along with Keating and the Archbishop and Mayor of Dublin, was subsequently instrumental in the crowning of Lambert Simnel – a Yorkist rival to King Henry VII, of the House of Tudor – as the short reigning King Edward VI, in Christ Church Cathedral on 24th May 1487 and the 'carrying of him from thence to the King's Castle upon tall men's shoulders', where he was formally installed.

On his death, his son Garret Óg succeeded as head of the House of Kildare and was appointed Lord Deputy a number of times during the following seventeen years. King Henry VIII was understandably very anxious to extinguish the power of this dynasty and in 1533 summoned Garret Óg to answer charges that he had furnished his own castles with armaments taken from Dublin Castle and that he had also 'supplied the wild Irish'. Garret Óg went to London, leaving his Chief Governor's duties to his twenty-one-year-old son Thomas, known as Silken Thomas, either because of the silk mantles or the silk plumes on his men's helmets. Henry then had false reports spread throughout Dublin that Garret had been executed in the Tower.

Silken Thomas reacted rashly to this incitement. He rode through the town on 11th June 1534, with a band of 140 armed horsemen, crossed the Liffey ford to the Chapter House of St. Mary's Abbey, where the King's Council was in session, and flung down his great sword of State in a dramatic act of defiance by which he hoped to force his claim to power. (Henry treated this action as open revolt and confined Garret Óg and his brothers to the Tower, where he died two months later.)

On leaving the Abbey, Thomas found that the citizens had slammed shut the town gates against him. He then took hostage some sons of town citizens that were being evacuated to safety and demanded entry into the town in order to attack the Castle. Archbishop Allen was an enemy of the Fitzgeralds and was believed to have carried the King's malicious story. He had sought refuge in the Castle, but, fearing for his safety, left in a small boat via the Poddle and transferred to a larger vessel on the Liffey. This ran aground on Clontarf Island. He was discovered later and Thomas handed him over to his followers who 'brained and hacked him in gobbets'. [18]

Advancements in artillery made even strong fortifications vulnerable and the town citizens had petitioned the King for six small defensive cannons – one for each of the main town gates – but they had yet to arrive. Constable John White, the chief security officer in charge of overall defence and guardian of works and supplies in the Castle, was informed of developments and had the following supplies delivered the night before the citizens agreed to Thomas's demands: 'Twentie tun of wine, four and twentie tun of beer, two thousand dried ling, sixteen hogsheads of salted beef, and twentie chambers [guns] with an iron chain for the draw-bridge of the castell.'[19]

below John Derrick's (standard pattern) woodcut of Silken Thomas's attack on Ship Street Gate, Dublin Castle. (From Holinshed's Chronicles of Ireland, 1577).

Thomas had the town's water supply cut off, so depriving it of power to drive the corn mills. After a short siege, with food and water supplies running low, the town surrendered and Thomas's troops entered through New Gate. His first assault was directed at Castle Gate, from vacant ground north of Isolde's Tower (see map p.35) with fire from three 'Falcon' cannons. However, these were too light and had little effect. (It is probable that these were the armaments that Garret Óg had been found guilty of removing from the Castle.)

Thomas was then sidetracked by his arch enemies, the Butlers, and on his return again found the city gates shut against him. Word had come from King Henry that help was on its way; the Castle garrison had raised the flag proclaiming that the truce was ended and the town citizens turned on the besiegers, many of whom were killed or imprisoned in the Castle.

His attack then switched to Ship Street Gate, but cannon fire from the Castle dislodged his men who also lost their defensive cover – 'all the adjacent thatched houses being at the same time burnt with wildfire by Constable White.' Finally, the storming and attempted arson of New Gate went disastrously wrong when the defenders charged out and scattered his men.

The promised relief forces under the newly appointed Lord Deputy, Sir William Skeffington (1530-32), landed in Dublin and marched on Maynooth Castle, which was immediately laid under siege. Thomas's foster brother, Warden Parris, betrayed the garrison, which was 'put to the sword' following agreement on surrender terms and the laying down of arms. This reneging on the agreement is still remembered as the 'Pardon of Maynooth'.

Other Fitzgerald Castles were then captured in succession and Silken Thomas surrendered on 24th August 1535. Three of his uncles, who had opposed his rebellion, attended a banquet at the invitation of Lord Deputy Leonard Grey (1535-40) and were delivered to Dublin Castle in chains. They, along with Thomas and his two other uncles, were transported to the Tower of London and were hung, drawn and quartered at Tyburn tree and their heads set on spikes on London Bridge, on 3rd February 1537.

The fall of the House of Kildare left the way open for the Tudor conquest – a new era in the history of Ireland.

Dublin's Medieval Towers, Walls & Streets

Dublin Castle:

THE UPPER CASTLE YARD, or Great Courtyard, today corresponds closely with the rectangular enclosure of the early thirteenth century Castle. The main hall of Dublin Castle Conference Centre is partly supported by the remains of the Corke Tower which can be seen from its roof garden. The butt of the Powder Tower and parts of the tenth century Viking town defence bank are on view at the Undercroft. The Record Tower is the last intact medieval tower, not only of the Castle but also of Dublin City.

Considerable sections of the old curtain wall are preserved under the present buildings and a 2.5m (8ft) thick section extends above ground along the length of St. Patrick's Hall. The base of the Bermingham Tower is original – the superstructure dating from 1777 – as are the remains of the adjoining Square Tower.

THE CORKE TOWER was three storeys, 19m (63ft) high with 3m (10ft) thick walls and included a

below Superimposition of outline of the medieval Castle on the modern Upper Castle Yard.

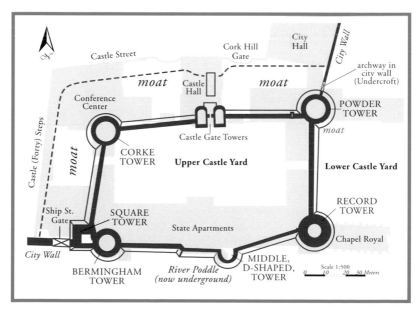

dungeon. As with all the others, it contained loopholes that enabled archers and gunners to direct flanking fire along the curtain walls towards the next tower and over the surrounding area. It and the adjoining east and north curtain walls bordered the town and three of its eight (and of the Castle's eighty) loopholes faced west and north.

However, the foundations had been built on boulder clay and it became structurally unsound. The huge explosion on Wood Quay in 1596 caused further damage. Lord Deputy Henry Falkland had made plans for its demolition but reported that, on the morning of 1st May 1624, it 'fell to the ground with the ordnance mounted upon it. The fall has shaken a great part of the wall, and it will cost much to replace, which had better be done at once, but money must be sent to do it with.' There were no fatalities.

The rebuilding works were completed in 1631 at the expense of the Lord Treasurer Richard Boyle, 1st Earl of Corke, whose Corke House mansion was adjacent to the Castle on the site of the former Church of St. Mary del Dam, which was closed during the Reformation. (This site is now occupied by City Hall.) He claimed that the works cost him £1,200 and that had it been carried out at the King's expense, 'it would not have been completed for £2,000'. A religiously

intolerant opportunistic adventurer, he had been imprisoned in the Castle a number of times during the 1590s for defrauding the State through falsification of records. His very cheap acquisition of vast estates from Sir Walter Raleigh made him one of the richest men in Ireland and his marriage (1603) to the daughter of the Secretary of the Irish Council brought him social respectability. In 1616 he was dubbed Baron of Youghal in a formal ceremony in the Castle.

He was also the champion of the 'New English' (and father of the scientist who formulated 'Boyle's Law') but was humiliated by Lord Deputy Wentworth, (see ch.12), who, in 1634 forced him to move the newly erected tomb of his wife from its prominent position in St. Patrick's Cathedral. However, the Earl later took revenge by being involved in the impeachment that led to his execution.

During archaeological excavations in the 1980s, a section of masonry was uncovered and the cross beams were found in a good state of repair. The base of this (1631) tower survived and remains exposed as an architectural feature.

CASTLE GATE, the town entrance, was a twin D-shaped guard house and prison block with portcullis (defensive grating) and was sited immediately west of the present Gate of Justice. As with the other towers, additional surveillance was provided by sentry patrols on the adjacent thick curtain walls, which were dotted with loopholes that could be manned in the case of attack.

In 1276, Hubert de Burgh and fellow prisoners burned part of one of these towers, causing damage amounting to fifty marks. The adjoining turnbridge (or horizontally pivoting drawbridge) was also repaired, at a cost of ten marks. In 1315, Justiciar Edmund Butler ordered the spiking of as many as possible of seventy severed (O'Mores') heads above the 2m (8ft) wide gateway. In 1572, Castle Gate was reported to be 'riven from top to bottom to the hazard of the porter and the prisoners lodged therein'. Extensive rebuilding works were completed in 1617.

Henry Fitzsimons, a Jesuit Priest, was jailed here between 1599-1604 (following which he was exiled). In his writings, he accused Constable Tristram Eccleston of having him closely watched to prevent him celebrating Mass. He made repeated attempts to attract the attention of passers bye, 'but they neither wished to look up at me in the tower, nor did they pretend to hear me, when from the castle or the cell I challenged them in a stentorian voice'.

It was from here that Red Hugh O'Donnell made his first escape by lowering himself onto the drawbridge (1592); where Peter Talbot, Catholic Archbishop of Dublin, died in custody (1680) and where Archbishop Oliver Plunkett was held in a 'costly and expensive apartment' for which he had to pay £1 per week, prior to his execution at Tyburn (1681).

Castle Gate was demolished in 1750 and a number of skulls were unearthed in the adjacent moat area during foundation works for the new Bedford Tower. Archaeological excavations in the 1980s uncovered the causeway, where massive foundations on both sides appear to have been the remains of a barbican, or projecting tower, which may have protected two drawbridges – one of which spanned half the distance, with the second completing the traversal of the Castle ditch.

THE CASTLE MOAT, ditch or fosse, was U shaped in outline, averaged 21m (69ft) in width and 8.5m (28ft) in depth and was largely quarried from the limestone bedrock. [20] The River Poddle (which flows eastwards under the Back Avenue and turns northwards near the eastern end of the Chapel Royal – see images p.35 and inside back cover) was dammed by a weir to provide a millpond for Dam's Mill (at Crane Lane, off Dame Street) and filled the north ditch –

which probably was replenished with Liffey water during spring tides. Only the western ditch remained dry, but it too was a formidable defensive feature of approximately 12m (40ft) width and 6m (19ft) depth. The moat also received the sewage discharge from the Castle latrines and was used as a convenient dump over the centuries.

THE POWDER TOWER
occupied a commanding position at the point where the Castle was joined by the eastern town wall. Here, the archway allowed small boats to land provisions, via the moat from larger vessels on the Liffey, at the set of steps cut through the curtain wall which gave access to the postern, sally port or minor gate.

(See current Undercroft p.128. In addition to a high water table, there is also some seepage through the blocked [c 1400] archway from the culverted Poddle, which enters the Liffey at Wellington Quay.)

There were eleven loopholes in this tower, of which seven flanked the north wall to the great gate, one scoured the north-west, another the north-east, two scoured the east wall, 'being the garden wall' and one other 'the garden eastwards'. The top or fifth floor was occupied by Lord Deputy Perrot in 1584 and contained two of the building's eight windows – 'the one east and the other north'.

THE RECORD TOWER was the mightiest of them all, with 4.6m

below State Apartments' garden frontage, with Octagonal Tower to left, State Apartments in centre, Record Tower and Chapel Royal to right and Dubhlinn Gardens in foreground.

(15ft) thick walls – much thicker than the other towers and very suited to its function as a top security jail for State prisoners. Tradition maintains that Red Hugh made his second and successful escape from here (see chapter 9). It was given many names over the centuries including Gunners' Tower and Wardrobe Tower and took its present name in 1814 – the time of its conversion to house the Public Records of Ireland – when the upper section was rebuilt, the floors and staircase were replaced and the battlements added to match the style of the adjoining new Chapel Royal.

THE D-SHAPED OR MIDDLE TOWER, in the southern curtain wall, was three storeys high with six loopholes for defenders to repulse attack from the south and to provide effective fire along the adjoining curtain walls. In 1689, 'fell down the mid rampier of the Black Clock Tower, with the fane on which was displayed the Crown and Regal Arms, which did no harm, only killed the sentry who was found dead among the rubbish'. The present Octagonal Tower is on its approximate site. There were ten loopholes and small windows in the curtain wall between here and Bermingham Tower.

THE BERMINGHAM TOWER had four levels, was of advanced military design and is likely to have been the first built by Justiciar de Londres. It adjoined a dungeon block and served as a prison as needs required. It was named after members of the Bermingham family, who were prominent in the colony during the early fourteenth century. John, Earl of Louth, served as Justiciar from August 1321 to the following February, during which time William, his brother, was his second-in-command. William was an associate of the 'treasonous' 1st Earl of Desmond and was arrested, along with his son Walter (1330), by Justiciar Anthony Lucy and imprisoned here. He was hanged and drawn for sedition in 1332, not-withstanding his 'great military services against the natives'. Walter later served two terms as Justiciar (1346 and 48).

Dr. Creagh, the Catholic Primate of Ireland, was jailed here in 1564 and described his cell as 'a hole where without candle there is no light in the world'. When occasionally he had use of a candle, it 'so filled with smoke, that had there not been a hole in the next door to draw in breath with my mouth set upon it, I had been perhaps shortly undone.' Three years later, a jailer named Walsh aided and abetted his escape, but he died in the Tower of London in 1585.

The State Records, including the Patent, Plea and Pipe Rolls where exchequer accounts were recorded, were stored here from 1537-1810. Following structural damage caused by an explosion in the nearby Armoury (1764), they were removed for safekeeping and the tower was taken down to its sloping base. It was rebuilt (1777) with three levels, thinner walls, and connected to the new Wedgewood (billiard) Room. A kitchen existed at lower ground floor level until the mid twentieth century and meat hooks can still be seen in the adjoining store.

THE SQUARE TOWER abutted the Bermingham Tower where the southern town wall crossed the Castle ditch. Three of its loopholes scoured the gardens southwards, two others westwards 'into the town' and two more flanked the west curtain wall towards Corke Tower. This small tower was reduced in height to form a gunnery platform – the remains of which are still visible.

Dublin Town

In all, thirty-two towers and gates formed part of the medieval walled town's fortifications (see opposite). The Corporation leased some to wealthy officials and merchants as fortified dwellings – with the right reserved for free access for town defence purposes – so ensuring that they were well maintained at no cost to the citizens. Many were named after their occupants or the purposes to which they were put.

Immediately outside the Castle's Ship Street Gate is a stretch of the town's southern walls that were 8.5m (28ft) high and 2.1m (7ft) wide. The town's 6-m (20ft) deep town ditch ran parallel to it, along what is now Little Ship Street, following the course of the River Poddle (as illustrated).

Here also is a substantial remnant of the STANYHURST TOWER, which was three storeys, 6m (20ft) high, with 1.8m (6ft) wide walls, and contained six loopholes for archers and gunners. It is named after James Stanyhurst, the local successful merchant lawyer, who was Mayor of Dublin, Recorder of the City and Speaker of the Irish House of Commons. He lived in the adjoining property, worked in the Castle during his time as Recorder and had been one of the boy hostages taken by Silken Thomas's men.

James's great-great-grandfather may have come to Ireland with King Richard II's first expedition (1394). His grandfather was a buyer of wheat, salt and iron, who, in 1470, became Bailiff and then Mayor of Dublin. His father, Nicholas, had also been Mayor and thereafter City Treasurer and Alderman. He repaired Pole Gate Bridge, which spanned the Poddle,

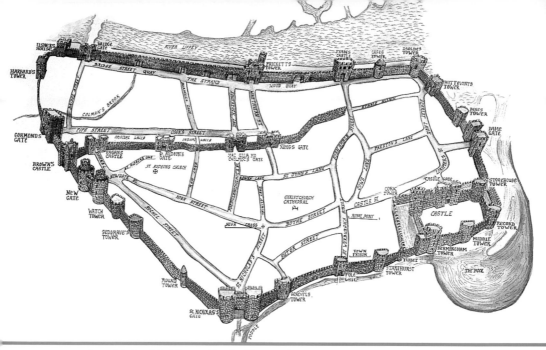

above Medieval Dublin, c.1500, by Christine Crotty.

and obtained the Priory of the White Friars after the dissolution of the monasteries.[21]

James's son, Richard, wrote *The Description of Ireland* especially for Hollinshed's *Chronicles* of 1577 (dedicating it to the Lord Lieutenant, Henry Sidney) which is our primary source of information on the Silken Thomas attacks. He later converted to Catholicism and escaped to the Court of King Philip 11, where he became a Royal adviser.

POLE GATE stood at the junction of present-day Werburg Street and Little Ship Street and was named after the Dubhlinn pool or harbour. Square shaped and two storeys high with prison vault and portcullis, its 2m (6ft) wide walls contained three loopholes and an inner yard of 4.25m² (14ft²). Together with the double, three-storey, ST. NICHOLAS GATE – the most southerly point of the town – it allowed access to the grazing fields, monastic houses and suburbs.

THE FAIR GREEN was located outside the town walls and dry ditch, from St. Nicholas's Gate to close to Sedgrave's Tower, and its fifteen day July fair was the town's major attraction. Stallholders were charged for their sites and visitors paid admission – all these proceeds went to the Lord Deputy while the Archbishop received the profits from the first two days trading.

Entertainment was provided by minstrels, jugglers, wild animal acts and street theatre. Spectators could participate in tug of war, wrestling and feats of strength. Scribes drew up deeds, wills and contracts for the mostly illiterate population and a number of languages would have been heard: Old English, Latin, Classical Irish and perhaps French, which would have been spoken by some of the nobility. [22]

On each feastday of Corpus Christi during the fifteenth and sixteenth centuries, following Mass in Christ Church, the self regulating Trade and Craft Guilds (which controlled the standard of workmanship, wages and prices) presented Miracle plays and pageants from classical mythology, on two-storey wagons that encircled the audience of Lord Deputy, Mayor and townspeople. Later, each was re-enacted in individual town streets. These often melodramatic, humorous or religious folk dramas were repressed during the Reformation. [23]

NEW GATE was constructed in 1177 on the site of the ancient settlement of Áth Cliath (see p.7) and comprised of two three-storey towers surmounted by turrets, with portcullis, murder-hole and loopholes. It guarded the intersection of the major long-distance roadways – including the *Slighe Mhór*, which continued through High Street and terminated at the Market (or High) Cross. (This was connected to Castle Gate by Skinners' Row [named Bothe Street until 1305 and currently Christ Church Place] and Castle Street).

It acted as the city prison from 1485 to 1794, when it was superseded by the Sheriff's Prison in Green Street. In 1526 it held seven prisoners – one incarcerated for trespassing, four for failure to pay debts and two for serious crimes. In 1608 it was surmounted by the impaled heads of Co. Donegal chieftains – trophies of Lord Deputy Chichester's campaigns in Ulster(p.56).[24] *The Chain Book* gives an inventory of its grisly contents. 'There were gyves, small bolts for the dungeons, legbolts with shackles, bolts with collars for men's necks, a pair of manacles weighing one stone and two bolts with small sized shackles for children.' Sentries also provided additional and constant vigilance from the nearby WATCH TOWER.

BROWN'S CASTLE at times housed a State prison and was a Marshalsea (or debtors) prison in the eighteenth century. The earlier town walls and associated ditch swung eastwards from here along the pre land reclamation shoreline. These stone walls were originally built by the Vikings in the early-twelfth century (replacing the encircling earthen banks) and were strengthened and improved by the Anglo-Normans in during the thirteenth century.

A large section of wall is visible at ST. AUDOEN'S GATE which, along with the adjacent, extant, Parish Church (1190), was intimately connected with the Trade and Craft Guilds. This became the Tanners' meeting hall in the fourteenth century and they took a ninety-nine-year lease in 1675 – the property then described as containing two rooms; one being over the other and 6m (20ft) by 5m (17ft) clear within the walls.

Following the granting of Catholic emancipation in 1829, the Municipal Corporation Reform Act of 1840 disbanded these medieval Guilds with one exception – the Goldsmiths – because they exercised control over the trade, prevented abuses by use of a recognised hallmark (signifying the standard for gold and silver) and collected duty on precious metals for the government. [25] Now known as the Assay Office, it celebrated the 350th anniversary of the granting of its reconstituted charter by King Charles I in 1987 – a history that has seen it move its hall from premises at Gormond's Gate to Werburg Street and from Golden Lane (to which it provided the name) to the former army-canteen building of the Castle's Ship Street Barracks.

TOWN STREETS and districts tended to become associated with particular commercial and industrial trades and activities and this was often reflected in their names – many of which, such as Cornmarket (inside New Gate, where there was a pillory and bear-bating ring), survive to this day.

In High Street (the former Viking comb makers' area) were meat stalls, eating-houses and leather works. Schoolhouse Lane, off High Street, still carries that name and had a State primary-level school for boys. (Education wasn't normally available to females.) The fish market was in Fishamble Street, while taverns sold wine and beer in Winetavern Street. In Castle Street, blacksmiths produced knives (universally carried), buckles, horseshoes and spurs. In Sheep (now Ship) Street, sheep and other animals were sold. In Cook Street were the bakeries – sited outside the earlier town walls because of the risk of fire, while tanneries were further afield.

Fines were imposed in cases of lack of hygiene, but, as there were no civic collections of domestic waste, the streets were dirty. Infant mortality was high and life expectancy only forty years. The standard of living was also low and possessions were few.

BRIDGE GATE, constructed in 1314, was well fortified to guard the only Liffey (Ostman or Dublin) bridge, which accommodated shops at that time, was destroyed in 1385 and rebuilt in 1428 by the Dominicans to serve their Priory of St. Michan's (the parish church of Oxmantown). A clock was fixed to the building in 1573, 'for regulating the motions of market people homewards' – thirteen years after the first three public timepieces were installed at the Middle Tower in the Castle, City Hall (the Tholsel) and St. Patrick's Cathedral. The Usher family, whose fortified house lay nearby and whose name lives on in the adjoining Ushers' Island and Quay, made repairs in 1595. Lord Lieutenant Whitworth laid the foundation stone for Whitworth (now Fr. Matthew) Bridge on this spot in October 1813.

The $2^2/_3$m (9ft) high town wall was interrupted in places along MERCHANT'S and WOOD QUAYS. Animal hides and wool, salted fish, grains, flax and timber were loaded for export and imports of wine, iron ore and salt were landed at the Crane of Dublin (with custom house in the upper room) alongside PRICKETT'S TOWER at Winetavern Street junction. The shallow depth of water in the Liffey channel and sand bars in the bay often necessitated large ships having to anchor in the deep harbour pools and transfer goods to smaller boats, or offload the heaviest cargoes at Dalkey Harbour and discharge the remainder at this crane.

During lunchtime on the 11th March 1596, 140 barrels of gunpowder, for use by Crown forces in the Nine Years' War, exploded here, while awaiting transportation to the Castle. Damage was extensive and was recorded in all areas of the walled town. 'No less than six score [120] bodies were identified besides sundrie headless bodies and heads without bodies, that were found and not known.'[26] These included a group of children, the entire family of the crane supervisor, Stephen Sedgrave, and the transport ship's captain, Mr. Ratlyfe of Chester.

Lord Deputy William Russell (1594-96) ordered the jailing in the Castle of John Allen, the overseer in charge of the unloading, who had been absent from duty 'supping a pot of beer', and the establishments of an official inquiry. The possibility of sabotage by civilians sympathetic to the rebels was excluded and the likely cause was identified as a spark from a nail in one of the barrels that the children had been rolling around. In 1621, Lord Deputy Henry Carey proudly announced that 'we have caused a

Custome house, Crane and Wharfe to be builded' on the recently reclaimed ground east of modern Parliament Street which was to be the 'only, sole and proper Crane and Wharfe for…goods…to be by sea exported or imported into or forth of this said Port of Dublin'. [27] Prickett's Tower had been irretrievably damaged by the explosion and was never rebuilt.

FYAN'S CASTLE on Blind Quay, at Fishamble Street junction, was four storeys high and named after Alderman Richard Fyan, who had it reconstructed. It housed a State prison in the seventeenth century and was demolished to make way for Essex Quay, which became operational in the early-eighteenth century.

Adjoining it was one of the city's three public privics (toilets) which discharged directly into the Liffey – the others being at Colman's Brook (beside Gormond's Gate) and on the east side of CASE'S TOWER – which became known as the Bakers' Tower after it was rebuilt, fortified and occupied by the Guild of Bakers in the early-eighteenth century.

The butt of the massive two-storey, circular ISOLDE'S TOWER can be seen today below ground level, beside the public house of the same name, in Lower Exchange Street. It was built during the late-thirteenth century on a prominent position to guard the confluence of the Poddle and the Liffey. Richard Stanyhurst claimed, in 1577, that it took the name from Isolde, 'daughter of Anguish, King of Ireland. It seemeth to have a castle of pleasure for the kings to recreate themselves therein.'

The Celtic love story of Tristan and Isolde is immortalized in Wagner's opera and Thomas Malory's *Morte d'Arthur* – the Arthurian Chronicles of the Round Table. Knight Tristan fell in love with Princess Isolde who was engaged to another: 'In every man's mouth it is, that Tristan was of love drunk.' Chapelizod (from the Irish *Séipéal Isolde* (Isolde's Chapel) straddles the Liffey on Dublin's western outskirts and is associated with this legend.

Here, the Lord Lieutenants, including Ormonde (thrice between 1643-85), Arran (1682-84), Capel (thrice 1672-95), Galway (1697-99), Grafton (thrice 1715-24) and Dorset (five times 1730-54), had their country residences – a welcome relief from the Castle air which was considered unhealthy because of the high walls and prisons. (The Countess of Arran wrote to her father in law in January 1683: 'I have found the air of the Castle soe close, that to seek a remedy for the ills it made me sensible of, I have been these two or three days at Chapellyzard'.)

Isolde's tower was leased in 1601 to Jacob Newman, who reclaimed part of the Poddle estuary and the Liffey bank. In 1620, King James I instructed Lord Deputy Oliver St. John to accept a lease from Mr. Newman of a place in the Port of Dublin 'which is found to be convenient for erecting a crane and making a wharf and in lieu thereof to grant him, for a term of 90 years, the sum of £50 per annum.' This negotiation led to the construction of a quay and customs' facility immediately downstream of present Grattan Bridge. [28]

BUTTEVANT'S TOWER was described, in 1585, as being an old square ruinous tower with a vault. It stood on firm ground in the Poddle's channel and was removed by Lord Lieutenant Essex in 1674 because of traffic congestion to and from the quays. BISE'S DEMI-TOWER was three storeys high, with lofts and five loopholes. Baron John Wise occupied it when he was assigned to the Court of the Exchequer at the Courts of Justice in the Castle. It was demolished during the construction of Parliament Street (see p.84).

DAME'S GATE TOWER, or East Gate (located at the present Palace Street-Dame Street junction) received its name from the dam across the Poddle that powered Dam's Mill (in the millpond at present-day Crane Lane. This was one of a number of mills on the Poddle, which some commentators described as a mill race, including King's Mill in the eastern ditch 'beneath the Castle walls' and Pole Mill immediately upstream of Stanyhurst's Tower, Little Ship Street.) This double tower gate, with portcullis, guarded the roadway eastwards to the Priory of All Hallows and most importantly, the river approach to the Castle, and Dubhlinn Harbour – as from here, the town wall carried over an archway that linked into the Powder Tower and allowed access into the moat (see image p.20).

A description of 'Riding the Franchises' (or town fringes) in September 1488, tells how the Mayor and his companions (including the Goldsmiths Guild which assembled at 'Christchurch meadow at 4 am, decently furnished with horse and arms' and two new silver trumpets) proceeded 'in good array, taking their way out of Dame's Gate, turning on the left hand of the strand and from hence straight forward to the longstone of the Steyne.' They then followed the coastline to Ringsend, where a rider flung a spear into the sea – so extending the civic jurisdiction and continued their circuitous ride of the town boundaries.

Dublin Castle and Tudor Conquest

Lord Deputy Grey inaugurated and supervised the Irish Reformation Parliament in 1537, which passed the Act of Supremacy that declared King Henry VIII, his heirs and successors, to be 'Supreme Head of the Irish Church'. The Reformation, which had been spreading through Europe, had officially arrived in Dublin. In the course of time, this new 'established' or State church was to win the allegiance of the majority of British people, but this was not to be the case in Ireland, as most of the population and the Gaelic-Irish and Old-English Lords refused to change. Consequently, a number of priests and friars were imprisoned in the Castle for refusing to take the oath of supremacy.

Archbishop Brown, the Augustinian Priest who married Henry and Ann Boleyn in 1533 – which caused the severing of Henry's connection to the Papacy – succeeded John Allen as Archbishop of Dublin. He set about the destruction of 'Romish relics and images' on a large bonfire at the town's Market Cross. Grey disliked Brown and his zealous 'reforming principles'. Henry, in turn, mistrusted Grey on account of his 'placatory religious views' and his

below Derrick's woodcut of Lord Deputy Sidney and troop of mounted pikemen riding out through Castle Gate and west along Castle Street.

Fitzgerald in-laws. Even though he had aggressively implemented the policy of military conquest and extracted submissions rather than peace treaties as he 'traversed the country each year battering down castles with his artillery train', he was recalled and beheaded on Tower Hill, for alleged treachery to the Crown.

Henry ordered the dissolution of the Irish monasteries and, over the next number of years, Lord Deputy St. Leger (1540-47) and Archbishop Brown presided over their distruction. The power of the great monastic houses had been in decline for almost fifty years, but continued to play an essential role in provision of educational and health services. All but one was acquired by government supporters, their churches pillaged and demolished and the auxiliary buildings used for practical purposes.

The Archbishop's Palace of St. Sepulchre (now Kevin Street Garda Station) was chosen by the Lord Deputy as his private residence. The citizens of Dublin were successful in their petition to the King, to award them the Priory of All Hallows as compensation for the 'ruin and decay that the said city sustained in breaking their towers, bridges, houses, leads of the conduits of the water in the [Silken Thomas] siege thereof.' Henry duly obliged and granted the Priory to the 'Mayor,

bailiffs, commons and citizens of Dublin and their successors forever', as a reward for their loyalty and support during the rebellion. It provided the site for the new University of Trinity College 'near Dublin' which his daughter, Queen Elizabeth I, declared was to be for 'the education, training and instruction of youths in the study of the liberal arts and in the cultivation of virtue and religion'. She bestowed a Royal charter upon it and an annual funding grant, to which Lord Deputy William Fitzwilliam (1588-94) added £200 from his own purse as a 'once off' donation. Dame (Dam) Street was constructed on the former ancient trackway known as Thingmote Street to connect it directly and conveniently to Castle Gate.

William Brabazon, the 'enterprising' Under Treasurer, obtained St. Thomas's Abbey, and a considerable amount of building material from many others – including that of the Nunnery of St. Mary de Hogges, at Hoggen Green, which was demolished and the materials transported to the Castle for repair works. This nunnery, which had been founded in 1156 by Dermot MacMurrough (see chapter 3), on a riverside site, now passed through many hands, including those of future Lord Deputies: Carey, Carew and Chichester. The Irish Parliament

Building was constructed here in 1729 and now houses the Bank of Ireland, College Green.

The Castle was now becoming the seat of a series of powerful and ambitious, experienced and able, Protestant-English Lord Deputies and the headquarters of a horde of officials, lawyers and freelance adventurers who came to benefit from the spoils of reformation and conquest. This was where the imminent colonisation of Ireland was plotted and from where it was overseen. Henceforth the term Dublin Castle came into general use as a metaphor for the English administration; the site became the prime symbol of English misrule in Ireland and 'Castle Catholics' became the standard term for a collaborator' [29]

Lord Deputy Sussex (1556-65) forced an act through Parliament, which empowered the 'Plantation of Leix (Laois) and Offaly' and authorised the imposition of martial law to assist with the colonisation. This allowed the Crown authorities total power over life and death and although normally applied only as a temporary emergency measure, proved to be so successful that he extended it to the whole country. Furthermore, it paid for itself, as those implementing it were entitled to one third of 'traitors' goods. Summary executions became commonplace, no section of society

above Official portrait of Henry Sidney.

was safe and the Irish Chieftains were powerless to protect their people. [30]

On 25th February 1570, Pope Pius V excommunicated Queen Elizabeth as a heretic and declared that her subjects owed her no allegiance, either temporal or spiritual. (Henry had been regarded as a schismatic). As a result, the allegiance of her Catholic 'subjects', both native Irish and Old English, became of major concern to the Crown.

It provided further stimulus for Henry Sidney – brother-in-law of Sussex and three times Lord Deputy between 1565-1578, to energetically pursue the offensive policies of his predecessors against the 'barbarous natives'. In a letter in 1576 to the Privy Council (the main executive and administrative State body which advised the Queen) he stated: 'I write not to your honours the name of each particular varlet that hath died since I arrive, as well by the ordinary course of the law and martial law, as flat fighting with them... But I do assure you, the number of them is great, and some of the best, and the rest tremble for the most part... Down they go in every corner and down they shall go.' The following year, fifty O'Mores of Laois were treacherously killed, having agreed to attend a parley with Crown officials at Mullaghmast, Co Kildare. The ambush had been carried out in accordance with a commission signed by Sidney on the 18th March and the main perpetrator was knighted. [31]

Richard Stanyhurst described the common practice of placing the decapitated heads of rebels on spikes over Castle Gate (see image p.41) as:

THOSE TRUNKLESS HEADS DO PLAINLY
SHOW EACH REBELS FATAL END
AND WHAT A HEINOUS CRIME IT IS,
THE QUEEN FOR TO OFFEND.

Angus O'Daly (1309–1350), the bard (professional poet and musician) to a Co. Wicklow chieftain killed in battle, viewed this 'Castle tradition' from a contrary standpoint:

O BODY WHICH I SEE WITHOUT A HEAD,
IT IS THE SIGHT OF THEE WHICH HAS
WITHERED UP MY STRENGTH.
DIVIDED AND IMPALED IN ÁTH CLIATH.

Sidney moved his household into the Castle, which had been neglected for almost 200 years and had become 'ruinous, foul, filthy and greatly decayed'. He initiated a huge building programme, that resulted in 'a verie faire house for the Lord Deputie or the Chief Govenor to reside and dwell in.' [32] By 1570, he had completed the Deputies House, with Clock Tower and Chapel, at the south wall of the Castle enclosure and a new Council Chamber at the north side. He was also responsible for extending and planting the Castle gardens, which included secure drawbridge access across the south ditch. Some alterations to the southern curtain wall, however, were viewed as creating a security weakness 'by the means of the hall windows and other windows with privies.'

Watson's plan of 1606 (as shown) indicates the location of the various Castle buildings, including those 'beautified and re-edified by Sidney' for the new throng of officials. The Council Chamber, Master of the Rolls and Offices of the Auditor were at the north wall. The Courts of Justice, clockwise from top left – Exchequer, Pleas, King's Bench and Chancery – were sited in the Great (or King's) Hall at the west wall. This 80ft (24m) by 120ft (36m) building also served as the Parliament House, which was perilously situated at first-floor level above the munitions store – 'a source of much complaint' – and had a separate postern gate entrance in the curtain wall which connected to a new bridge spanning the ditch.

Sidney's health had suffered from the Irish campaigns and for him, the post of Lord Deputy had been a thankless job. No one called into question his military record, but the Queen felt that he was too ambitious and, following complaints from the colony about his domineering behaviour, she charged him with squandering her money and recalled him in 1578. This was an injustice as he had spent so much of his personal fortune in Ireland that his son depended on Henry's brother for maintenance. He was profoundly disappointed and aggrieved at not securing more recognition for a lifetime of service and described himself as being 'fifty-four years of age toothless and rambling and £5,000 in debt.' [33] During retirement he became increasingly disillusioned with England's 'Irish Policy' and circulated papers criticising it.

The 'New English' of Queen Elizabeth's colonial administration saw Ireland and its natives as a territory and a population to be conquered and civilised – much as the Spanish Conquistadors of the same century viewed South America.[34] The Attorney and Solicitor General, Sir John Davies, (1569-1626) epitomised their attitude and determination: 'A barbarous country must first be broken by war before it will be capable of good government.' Arbitrary, full scale colonisation was his stated goal and he directed his energetic zeal towards the dismantling of the traditional Brehon legal system. He also publicly criticised previous Chief Governors who 'did not abolish the Irish customs, nor execute the law in the Irish counties but suffered the people to worship their barbarous lords and to remain utterly ignorant of their duties to God and the King'

Widespread religious persecution caused the once unimaginable to happen and the Old-English Catholics and the Gaelic Irish – their long time bitter enemies –

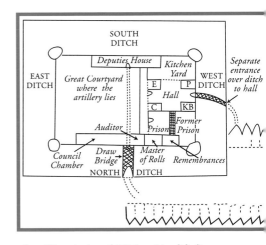

above Watson's plan of 1606AD. (simplified)

joined forces. The 'Plantation of Munster' provoked widespread rebellion and there were no less than six separate uprisings in a short space of time. Sir John Perrot, President of Munster, subjected the province to a reign of terror, systematic war and a policy of scorched earth that displaced much of the population. He boasted that he had killed more than 800 rebels in less than two years. As Lord Deputy (1584-87) he presided over Parliament at the confiscation of the Desmond lands.

The short, eventful, rule of Lord Deputy Arthur Grey de Wilton (1580-82) was 'marked by merciless severity and massacres that spared neither woman nor child.' He over-stretched himself however and was ambushed and defeated at the Wicklow Mountains' stronghold of Fíach MacHugh O'Beirne, who then burned the southern suburbs of Dublin. But he successfully foiled a conspiracy to seize the Castle and hung forty-five rebels in Dublin alone. O'Beirne's head was spiked above Castle Gate in 1597.

The poet, 'gentle' Edmund Spenser, spent nine years in the Castle as Secretary to the Lord Deputies, where he embarked upon his verse masterpiece 'The Faerie Queene' (which can be read as an allegorical demand for more draconian policies in Ireland) and wrote a proposal for the extermination of the Irish race. He summed up the horror of those times and the futility of the final days of conquest, where each side traded atrocity for atrocity: 'Why must it go on? – Because it has already gone too far!' [35] (He obtained planted lands in Co. Cork, but was ejected by the former owners and died in poverty in London). The 'holy war' did end, but not the hostility of the Old English and Gaelic Irish, whose unity in common cause was to endure.

Queen Elizabeth wrote to her Lord Deputy in jubilant mood: 'The mighty hand of the Almighty's Power hath showed manifestly the force of his strength in the weakness of the fairer sex.' By the end of her reign (1603) the country had been totally conquered and the Castle had become in reality the centre of English government and administration in Ireland, the full-time residence of the Chief Governor and the meeting place of the Council and the Courts of Law.

Mortal Combat and the Dark Side of Dublin Castle

In 1583, shortly after the Desmond rebellion, Conor McCormac and Tadhg McGilpatrick were involved in a dispute which ordinarily would have been would have been resolved by feud. As this would have violated the truce, Conor resolved to test the law and submitted his quarrel to the courts. He approached the Lord Chief Justice, who recommended that he press charges. Tadhg, the accused, travelled to Dublin Castle where he in turn was persuaded to bring charges of high treason against Conor. It was further decreed that mortal 'hand to hand combat' was the proper remedy.

At 9 am the following morning, before they could change their minds, they were paraded into the Castle courtyard which had been decorated in medieval tournament fashion. The Lords Justice were seated on a dais and the galleries were crowded with military officers, administrators, their wives and the leading citizens of Dublin.

The combatants were stripped to their waists and each armed with only shield, sword and skullcap. The trumpet sounded and the contest began. After some minutes hesitation, they were warned that their lack of action mocked the Queen's justice and that either they fought to the death to prove their innocence or both would be executed forthwith. The struggle began in earnest. Conor, the smaller of the two, was wounded twice in the leg and once in the eye and found his adversary too strong for him. Tadhg, who had held back, received a slash to the ribs. Enraged, he struck a series of blows that beheaded his opponent. He then presented Conor's head on the point of his sword to the Lords Justice.[36]

Tadhg and Conor were denounced as traitorous fools by their own people and the Gaelic world resolved to observe their own Brehon laws and avoid the Queen's Bench.

The Parliament that assembled in the Castle two years later (1585) passed a statute making Catholic priests and seminarians guilty of treason merely by being in Ireland. The possibility of religious pogroms was ever present and Mass houses and secluded Mass rocks soon began to appear in all areas. The Castle authorities viewed newly ordained priests returning to Ireland from mainland Europe as fulfilling the dual role of pastor to their flock and agitator for the religious Counter Reformation. Some of them were.

This was the political climate that Dermot O'Hurley, Catholic Archbishop of Cashel, encountered on his return during the autumn of 1583, from his position of Dean of Law in Louvain. He was recognised in the company of Thomas Fleming, Baron of Slane, and was reported to the Council in Dublin Castle by Fleming's first cousin, Sir Robert Dillon, Chief Justice of the Common Pleas. Fleming, who was now under accusation of treason (punishable by death) hurried after the Archbishop, caught up with him at Carrick-on-Suir and pleaded with him to go and clear his name. O'Hurley, under moral obligation, did the unthinkable and walked in to the Castle on the 8th October, where he was immediately arrested and imprisoned.

The unimaginable horror of imprisonment in chains in the Castle, that 'dark dismal and fetid prison' became his 'living hell' for the next eight months.[37] He was interrogated under cruel torture – his legs boiled in oil. But, he had no information to give. Lord Deputy Perrot (who lived in the top storey of the Powder Tower) signed the writ of execution on 19th June 1584. O'Hurley was hanged on the public gallows at Hoggen Green, early next morning.

At that time, Mrs Margaret Bell, a seventy-seven-year-old widow, was dying in the Castle. She was a committed Old-English Catholic, who had been 'discovered' attending Mass in her own home. Her eldest son Walter, Mayor of Dublin, had her arrested and publicly pulled through the streets on a horse-drawn wooden hurdle (wicker screen) as she was unable to walk. The conditions of this, her second imprisonment in the Castle, proved too harsh for her failing health. She died in 1584, following three years of captivity, and was buried in the family tomb in St. Audoen's Church.

A great absurdity was that prisoners had to pay for their own imprisonment – including meals and accommodation. Those rich enough could have their servants attend them and hostages were valued as profitable leverage tools to force concessions, including ransom or prisoner exchange and so, ordinarily fared well. However inability to pay necessitated dependence on charity and the meagre donations of Parliament. In effect, this often led to near starvation and postponement of release dates until debts were settled.

Perrot was directly responsible for the incarceration of the majority of the twenty political hostages, three priests and a bishop (Maurice O'Brien) held in the cells at this time. Countess Eleanor of Desmond was the widow of Gerald Fitzgerald, the former Earl whose death on 11th November 1583 ended the rebellion in Munster. She and her children spent eight months imprisoned there and she wrote afterwards that they endured extreme want and were almost starved. On occasion, the Lord Deputy took pity on them and sent them a dish from his table. One of her sons, an eight-year-old boy who later was to continue his 'service to the Crown' as a hostage in the Tower of London, wrote this sad note from his cell:

I AM YOUNG, YET OLD IN MISERY; I HAVE NEVER, SINCE MY INFANCY, BREATHED OUT OF PRISON.

He died in 1601, not long after his release from twenty-two years' imprisonment.

Perrot had made many powerful enemies on account of his notoriously bad temper and his vigorous application of personal policy. He was recalled and executed for treason in the Tower of London in 1592, even though he was an illegitimate son of Henry VIII and the evidence against him had been fabricated by his corrupt successor, Fitzwilliam. His reputation was restored thirty years later.

The Great Armada

As the first in a series of military strikes during Catholic King Philip 11 (Felipe de Habsburg) of Spain's undeclared war with Protestant Tudor England, he sent a huge naval war fleet to the Straits of Dover in 1588. Their over - ambitious plan was to protect a Spanish army crossing the Channel from Belgium and to join with them in an invasion of England. Drake's fireships scattered their defensive crescent formation at Gravelines and the 'invincible armada' was fortunate to escape without being blown aground. But, unable to turn back into the English Channel, it sailed before the strong prevailing wind and retreated up the North Sea, to take the difficult anti-clockwise route around Britain and Ireland.

Many ships were wrecked rounding the coast of Scotland and, having thrown overboard all their horses to conserve water, they took the long starboard course for Galicia. Their sailing orders, which were issued to each ship, included the instruction that they take great care to avoid the island of Ireland for fear of the harm that could happen upon the coastline. This was good advice, but the west coast of Ireland extends 80km (50 miles) further into the Atlantic than their navigational charts showed and moreover, some navigators mistook Achill Head, Co. Mayo for Cape Clear – the most southerly landfall. These factors, in addition to two weeks of prolonged south-westerly storms, battle-damaged vessels and

crews weakened by hardship, hunger, thirst and disease, proved fatal for the thirty ships and estimated 9,000 men that perished on that rugged coast. Some vessels, such as the great Mediterranean carracks, were simply unsuitable for the stormy conditions of the North Atlantic and were run aground on reefs or smashed to pieces against cliffs as they tried to find shelter in bays and inlets.

Lord Deputy Fitzwilliam who 'specialised in financial affairs and war', was not to know that the armada was already a spent force and reacted with raging fury to the news that the fleet was offshore. His immediate aim was to prevent the Irish joining forces in rebellion, in order to preserve the rare interval of peace – 'the tranquillity of exhaustion'. So, he spread a false report that 10,000 English troops were on the verge of landing at Dublin. Next, he issued a proclamation that all shipwrecked Spaniards must be handed over within four hours of detection and that failure to do so, or harbouring these enemies of the Crown, would be punishable by death 'on the spot'. He also instructed his regional governors to apprehend and kill all Spaniards 'of whatever social status' and that, as required, 'torture be used in prosecuting inquiry'.

The shipwrecked castaways suffered a variety of fates. All those in English hands or delivered into English hands were immediately killed. In Galway, Fitzwilliam discovered a group being held captive for ransom and personally directed their execution. Some Irish did rob those fortunate enough to have survived shipwreck. Contrary to the propaganda spread by the English Government – that the Spanish were spontaneously murdered by the Irish for their clothes, weapons and jewellery – there is only one recorded incident of the killing of Spanish castaways by Irish not directly in English pay and it provoked considerable local anger. Usually, they sheltered the Spanish and supplied their necessities. [38]

Red Hugh O'Donnell, son of Black Hugh, the chieftain of one of the leading clans of Ulster, had been lured onboard an English ship at Rathmullen the previous year, on the pretext of purchasing wine, and held hostage in Dublin Castle to guarantee the good behaviour of his father. Black Hugh proved to be an exception to the general rule as he marched some Spanish prisoners to the Castle to exchange for his son.[39] However, Fitzwilliam wouldn't trade and the chieftain's unscrupulous actions failed to secure either the release of or better treatment for Red Hugh. Tirlough Lynagh was infuriated by his kinsman's behaviour, promptly sent fifty cattle to relieve the hungry Spaniards in Ulster and was prepared to make war on O'Donnell in retribution – an allegation that Governor Richard Bingham, the 'Flail of Connaught', was quick to communicate to the Lord Deputy.

One of the few shipwrecked survivors was Captain Francisco de Cuellar, of the 'San Pedro'. He was protected by Brian O'Rourke of Breifne, of whom he wrote: 'Although this Chief is a savage, he is a good Christian and an enemy of the heretics and is always at war with them.' O'Rourke paid for his generosity with his life. Fitzwilliam had him hunted down and executed in the Tower of London. De Cuellar made a successful getaway through Scotland (which was not involved in the war) and had a further narrow escape in an ambush off the coast of the Netherlands, before returning home safely. [40]

The remaining sixty-eight ships of the armada 'limped home' to safety, but with many of their crews suffering from typhus and scurvy, they became a serious burden on Santander, Laredo and the other harbour towns that were already lacking in food and medicine.

The psychological effect of the defeat was devastating for Imperial Spain and marked the beginning of the end of her position as a world power. Less than ten years later, her treasury was empty and the Crown bankrupt. Philip would still not make peace in his crusade against 'heretical' Queen Elizabeth and dispatched two smaller armadas in 1596 and 97 – both of which were driven back by storms.

The war ended in stalemate following Philip's death, the surrender and repatriation of troops of the final armada (after the Battle of Kinsale) and the consequential policy shift by King Philip 111 which resulted in the peace Treaty of London, 1604. The anxiety and vulnerability of the Castle administration also ended with this battle – the result of which ensured, beyond doubt, the success of their conquest.

CRed Hugh and Gaelic Ireland's Last Stand

The kidnapping of Red Hugh O'Donnell had been carried out on the orders of Lord Deputy Perrot, who was alarmed at his engagement to the daughter of neighbouring Chieftain Hugh O'Neill and the consequential likelihood of the traditional enemies uniting. Three years later (1591) eighteen-year-old Red Hugh escaped from Castle Gate prison with two others, by climbing down a rope onto the drawbridge.

They made good their escape to the apparent safety of Phelim O'Toole's stronghold in the Wicklow Mountains. Phelim, who himself had been a prisoner in the Castle, reconsidered his situation as he feared the inevitable vengeance of Fitzwilliam. So, he handed them over to the authorities, who, according to tradition, 'confined them for more rigorous treatment' in the high-security Record Tower.

This was but one of many such attempted breakouts around that time. Thirteen hostages and 'other malefactors' had escaped five years previously and in 1588, twenty-two made a mass escape – eleven of whom were recaptured. A priest fell to his death in 1596 and five years later, jailer John Cole was granted a pension following injuries received in preventing escaping prisoners leaving the precincts.

On 6th January 1592, Red Hugh, along with Art and Henry O'Neill, sons of the Ulster Chieftain – who were also being held as hostages – took advantage of the guards 'in the very beginning of the night'. They unshackled their leg and wrist irons and, by means of a long rope, escaped through the privy conduit into the icy water of the moat and left the town before curfew. (This was shortly before Red Hugh was due to be transported to the Tower of London and Queen Elizabeth let it be known that she was convinced it was achieved 'by practice of money bestowed on somebody'.)

Again Hugh headed for the

Wicklow Mountains – this time to Fíach Mac Hugh O'Byrne's valley stronghold of Glenmalure. They became separated from Henry in the darkness, but made satisfactory progress until forced to shelter from a blizzard under a cliff overhang, while their servant pressed onwards to seek help. Their rescuers had difficulty finding them under the snow in the bleak bogland and believed them to be dead as they were only scantily clothed in light linen tunics, having left their 'coverlets and overmantles' in the privy. Art died of exposure, but, apart from losing his two big toes from frostbite, Red Hugh made a full recovery. (This, the most famous of all the escapes, is commemorated annually with a hike by Dublin ramblers along the route.)

O'Byrne supplied a troop of horses, enabling Hugh to evade capture by the English soldiers specially posted at the River Liffey crossings and return to Donegal, where he assumed leadership of the O'Donnell clan – his father being senile. He was quickly called into military action as Fitzwilliam sent a large military expedition into Ulster (the least anglicised province). The O'Donnell and O'Neill Clans united in open revolt, were armed by Old-English merchants and fought the guerrilla-like Nine Years War (1593-1603). A report in the Calendar of State Papers of

October 1597 described how 'the rebels rage all over the Pale so that almost no part of it is free from their killings, burnings, preying and despoiling.' They almost succeeded in their goal when they dramatically defeated an English army, inflicting 1,500 casualties, at the Battle of the Yellow Ford (14th August 1598) – a defeat that 'shook the Dublin administration till it tottered'.

Dublin's normal compliment of 1,200 armed soldiers was seriously depleted and the town left inadequately defended, as many had been sent to the war. Rebels burnt the suburbs of Kilmainham and Crumlin and conducted cattle raids around St. Patrick's Cathedral.

Robert Devereux, Earl of Essex and the Queen's favourite, volunteered to rectify the 'Irish problem' and was 'sworn in' as Lord Lieutenant in Dublin Castle on 15th April1598. However, the required ships were not made available for his intended seaborn expedition to Co. Donegal and he had a near disastrous six months term of duty, in which he ineffectively commanded his 16,000 strong army – the best equipped ever sent to Ireland. He was recalled, attempted to explain his actions and inactions in a 'face-to-face showdown' with Queen Elizabeth, at Nonsuch Palace, Surrey, and was executed in 1601.

Following their victories, the rebel army of 6,800 men under Hugh O'Neill and Red Hugh O'Donnell force- marched south to Co. Cork, where a Spanish expeditionary force of 3,400, under Don Juan del Águila, had landed on 21st September and was put under siege by the 8,000 strong army of Lord Deputy Mountjoy (1599-1603). The last stand of Gaelic Ireland took place in the early hours of Christmas morning 1601, when they were routed in open warfare at the Battle of Kinsale. The Spaniards blockaded in the town weren't aware of developments and didn't take part. Thus ended all hope of reversing the Tudor conquest.

O'Donnell fled to Spain in an attempt to get millitary support from Philip 111, who for monetary and strategic reasons was unwilling to dispatch a further armada. He died in mysterious circumstances at Simancas in August 1602, aged thirty years, and is said to have been poisoned by James Blake – the government agent. His body was removed to Valladolid (where the King held court) and was buried with full state honours at the Monastery of San Francisco.

O'Neill, a hunted man, submitted to Mountjoy on 30th March 1603 and signed the Treaty of Mellifont – so officially ended the Nine Years' War. He was taken to Dublin Castle, where he received a pardon and was informed that the Queen had died six days earlier. He is reported to have been 'unable to hold back his tears'.

False stories and rumours began to spread about him and his allies, including an anonymous letter (written by Baron St. Lawrence of Howth) which incriminated him in plotting the assassination of the new Lord Deputy Chichester. Fearing for their lives, O'Neill and Rory O'Donnell (newly elected Chieftain and brother of Red Hugh) gathered their families, friends and supporters and sailed from Rathmullen to the mainland of Europe in September 1607. This sorrowful exodus of the great Chieftains, known as the 'Flight of the Earls', marks the beginning of the modern history of Northern Ireland and is commemorated in a painting in the King's Bedroom, State Apartments.

Successive generations of poets, and bards deprived of their traditional patronage, have grieved the death of the age old Gaelic-Irish civilisation – such as Aindrais MacMarcuis in *This Night Sees Ireland Desolate:* [41]

HER CHIEFS ARE GONE.
THERE'S NONE TO BEAR
HER CROSS OR LIFT HER FROM DESPAIR;
THE GRIEVING LORDS TAKE SHIP. WITH
THESE OUR VERY SOULS PASS OVERSEAS.

The End of an Era

The 'Flight of the Earls' was a total disaster for the Gaelic Irish, whose Chieftains had been their main protection against foreign domination and assimilation. The Earls were convicted of high treason *in absentia* and their Clan lands declared forfeit to the Crown.

Lord Deputy Arthur Chichester (1603-1613) saw his opportunity for immediate removal of the inhabitants and their replacement with 'loyal subjects'. He put this plan to the English Council in 1607 and it was accepted. Two years later, the 'Articles of Plantation' were issued, which declared that the majority of Irish Catholics should be removed to specially designated areas – an idea similar to that of the later North-American Indian reservations.

The lands of Counties Donegal, Fermanagh, Tyrone, Derry and Armagh were targeted for colonisation. Derry – from the Irish *doire*, meaning oak wood – was granted to the City of London Guilds and the charter allowed the prefix 'London' to be added. (The use of either name, Derry or Londonderry, still signifies political allegiance.) This 'Plantation of Ulster' was on a greater scale than had previously been attempted and

proved to be permanent. The land was distributed and garrisoned as follows: 2,000 acres each to senior grantees on which they were required to build a castle. 1,500 acres each to those deserving English who had served the Government and on which they had to enclose their house with a bawn (defensive enclosure) and 1,000 acres each to 'deserving Irish'. [42] Thirteen thousand lowland Scots settled in these 'new lands'.

Chichester – who became founder and first Baron of Belfast – stated in his 'notes of remembrance' that he had killed all the native Irish he encountered irrespective of sex or rank. He also diligently jailed clerics in Dublin Castle, two of whom – Bishop Conor O'Devany and Fr. Patrick O'Loughran (former chaplain to Hugh O'Neill) were subsequently found guilty of treason in a show trial and were hung drawn and quartered in the presence of a large crowd on Oxmantown Green, 1st February 1612. His purpose in inflicting such severe treatment was not only to terrorise the clergy and population into converting to the State church, but also to intimidate the Old English Catholic controlled Parliament into passing penal laws. This backfired as King James 1 refused to sanction the proposed anti-Catholic legislation, and (as he [Chichester] wrote) O'Devany and O'Loughran were 'thought martyrs and adored ever since'.

Following the manipulation of electorate constituencies by the government – which reversed the balance of power and created a large Protestant majority – the Lord Deputy convened the highly confrontational Parliament of 1613 in Dublin Castle. The Catholic lords walked out in protest, but a commission of inquiry rejected their complaints of gerrymandering and Chichester (who headed that commission) declared their fears for personal safety, in the presence of the greatly strengthened Castle garrison, to be baseless. He also announced that they had no reason for impeding the sitting of Parliament "saving that which sticks so long in them – the doctrine of Rome and the dregs of Anti Christ". The Parliament reconvened with Catholic membership in attendance. Chichester later urged co-existence and was recalled for not being energetic enough in his repression of Catholics.

The grievances of the dispossessed Irish festered, intensified and erupted in the 1641 Rebellion. It commenced in Ulster where more than eighty Protestants were killed at Portadown Bridge (and possibly 12,000 in all during the rebellion. These atrocities sent a shock wave through the Ulster Protestant community that is still remembered today.)

The Old English of the Pale joined with the Gaelic Irish and a 'Catholic Confederation' army marched on Dublin and came very close to capturing it. More than eighty armed would-be attackers assembled at Oxmantown with the intention of carrying out a mass assault on Castle Gate the following morning, 23rd October. Their plan appears to have had a realistic chance of success as the garrison was under-strength (and the portcullis had been removed more than fifty years previously). However, the plot was betrayed at an Inn on Winetavern Street, the 'Parliamentarian' Lord Deputy William Parsons had the leaders arrested and so, the attempted seizure was thwarted.

The Castle garrison was strengthened by volunteer townspeople (who traditionally assisted the colony in times of necessity) who were now fully armed from the Castle's stockpile of 10,000 weapons, 35 pieces of artillery and 1,500 barrels of gunpowder. Refugee families from the Pale and Ulster sought refuge in the town as local Catholics were disarmed and expelled. The nationwide military crisis largely abated following the arrival in Dublin of large numbers of reinforcements from England, in 1642.

Control of the English army in Ireland proved to be the spark that ignited open conflict between the English Parliament and Charles I, King of England, Scotland and Ireland in the English Civil War. Some Old-English Catholics were tortured in the Castle (in the presence of two commissioners from the English Parliament) in the hope of creating a tenable connection between the aims of the Catholic Confederation and the Royalist cause. A Confederation army, which supported Charles, defeated an English army at Benburb in 1646, but the King was beheaded three years later.

Oliver Cromwell became the first 'commoner' Lord Lieutenant on his appointment by the English Parliament in 1649. Following disembarkation at Dublin Bay with an invasion force of 20,000 soldiers and a huge artillery train, he made the Castle his administrative base and 'was received with all possible demonstrations of joy, the great guns echoing forth their welcome and acclamation in every street'. During his nine months in Ireland, he unleashed a ferocious campaign of terror and persecution in which the 4,000 townspeople of Drogheda and Wexford were massacred, although they hadn't been part of the Confederacy. It was, he wrote, 'a righteous judgement of God upon those barbarous wretches, who have imbued their hands in so much innocent blood.' In 1658, his body was disinterred at Westminster Abbey and, with great ceremony, symbolically executed. Although he portrayed himself as a providential liberator, his demonised legend as oppressor endures in Ireland.

The country had been proclaimed completely subdued on 26th September 1653. Two years later Oliver's fourth son, Henry, was appointed Lord Lieutenant (for a four-year term). He continued his father's policies of transplantation of 'disloyal Irish' to Connaught, the least fertile Province, and the shipping of clergy and prisoners of war to slavery in the West Indies. He also authorised the seizure and transportation of 1,000 females 'for their own good', and 2,000 boys as 'who knows but it might be a means to make them Englishmen'. In April 1656, his son was christened in St. Patrick's Cathedral: 'the sermon and sacrament being ended, my lord, with this magnificent retinue, returned to the castle, where was an entertainment provided…which had its exit in a handsome banquet'.

The English monarchy was restored under Protestant Charles

II (son of Charles I) who was succeeded by his Catholic brother James II, in 1685. The Dutch, Protestant, Prince William of Orange (son-in-law of Charles I) was invited to lead a expedition against James, which he readily accepted as he was particularly anxious to secure consistent English support for the Dutch against the French[43] and was crowned King William III.

King James fled and in March 1689, on the urgings of Louis XIV who was then at war with the Netherlands, landed at Kinsale with the intention of using Ireland as a springboard from which to regain his Crown. He arrived triumphantly in Dublin on the 24th, accompanied by 6,000 French soldiers and French, Jacobean and Irish officers. They entered through St. James's Gate with Lord Deputy Tyrconnell to the forefront displaying the sword of State, while forty dancing women ran alongside the parade, through streets freshly covered with gravel and lined with soldiers of the garrison. Upon reaching the Castle, James dismounted and was accompanied into the Chapel to witness the singing of a 'Te Deum' in his honour. Then he withdrew to his new accommodation in the State Apartments, where he 'dined and refreshed himself.'

His duties included the bestowal of Trinity College on the English Jesuits (ensuring continuance of Royal control) and the imprisonment of the Dean of St. Patrick's Cathedral imprisoned in the Record Tower. On the 7th May, he proceeded in full procession from the Castle to the King's Inns, where he convened Parliament, presided over the reversal of the Act of Settlement and the resolution that the Parliament of England could not legislate for Ireland. For a brief time, Ireland possessed a complete and independent government. [44]

James now controlled most of the country, but on 7th December the Presbyterian defenders of Derry refused to accept him as their monarch and slammed the gates against the approaching 'Redshanks'. Non-combatants were allowed to leave and the now famous siege began. During the next 105 days, starvation and disease crippled the town. Eventually the siege was lifted by the 'hesitant' ship, the *Mountjoy*, which crashed through the boom across the River Foyle. Unfortunately, the courageous garrison never received its wages and many of them died in debt. 'No surrender!' has remained the catchword of Protestant Ulster ever since.

King William came in pursuit and landed at Carrickfergus on 4th November. With a force of 36,000 soldiers – comprising English, German, Dutch and Danes as well as Ulster Protestants and French Huguenots who had fled the persecutions of Louis XIV – they defeated King James's army of 25,000 troops at the Battle of the Boyne on 12th July 1690. James reached Dublin in advance of his bedraggled regiments and spent the night in the Castle before returning to exile in France. An often-repeated anecdote states that on complaining to Lady Tyrconnell that his cowardly Irish soldiers had run away, she replied: "it appears that your Majesty has won the race".

Two battalions of the Dutch Guard secured the town and Protestant Dublin again rejoiced, while William almost certainly held court at the Castle – which he made his official residence. Pope Innocent XI, an enemy of Louis XIV, ordered a 'Te Deum' to be sung in celebration of the glorious victory, in St. Peter's Basilica.

The war ended a year later, following the deaths of 10,000 Irish troops at the Battle of Aughrim. The resultant Treaty of Limerick guaranteed the rights and property of the defeated in return for their loyalty. The seventeenth century, which had opened with the crushing defeat at the Battle of Kinsale and the tragic 'Flight of the Earls', came to a close with what is known as the 'Flight of the Wild Geese', when 20,000 fighting men – the only effective protectors of native rights – sailed into exile in government-provided ships. These were the forerunners of a great exodus of fighters that continued for a century and formed the Irish Brigades in the armies of Spain, France, Netherlands, Austria, Poland and Russia. 'Remember Limerick!' was their battle cry.

Few ever returned, but folklore fancifully supposed that, following death in battle, their souls came back to Ireland in the form of migrating geese. Emily Lawless captured the stark reality of life for many of them: [45]

below 'Flight of the Wild Geese'

WAR-BATTERED DOGS ARE WE,
FIGHTERS IN EVERY CLIME,
FILLERS OF TRENCH AND OF GRAVE,
MOCKERS, BEMOCKED BY TIME,
WAR-DOGS, HUNGRY AND GREY,
GNAWING A NAKED BONE,
FIGHTERS IN EVERY CLIME,
EVERY CAUSE BUT OUR OWN.

*O*ppression, Dissension & Dispossession

above ¹/₂ *actual size. The penal cross is unique to Irish folk art. The arms are short to allow it be hidden up the sleeve. The cock and pot symbolised the resurrection.*

The agreed terms of the Treaty of Limerick were quickly contravened. Every session of the Irish Parliament from 1695 to 1746 brought into law draconian measures against Catholics, known as the penal laws. Their purpose was to exclude 'Papists' from political life, dispossess them of their remaining lands and encourage religious conversions.

The 1704 Popery Act discriminated against all non-Anglicans. Presbyterians, Quakers and other 'dissenters' were treated less severely than Catholics, in that their land holdings and succession rights were unaffected. However, they bitterly resented trade embargoes, compulsory Anglican tithes and exclusion from 'any office, civil or military, or receiving any pay or salary from the Crown, or having command or place of trust from the sovereign'. Many thousands emigrated to the New World of the North American colonies.

Lord Lieutenant Simon Harcourt (1772-77) wrote that 'the Presbyterians in the North are in their hearts American'. Eleven Presidents of the United States were descendants of Ulster Protestant, mostly Presbyterian, pioneers – as were Davy Crockett and Elvis Presley. [46]

above Sculpture of Jonathan Swift, sited
over the main entrance to the Chapel Royal.

The Banishment Act of 1697
had exiled all Catholic Bishops,
required registration of resident
priests and forbidden replacements
'under pain of death'. Rewards were
offered to priests to convert and £5
paid per capita to 'priest catchers'.
Other Acts barred Catholics from
attending Catholic worship and
schools, and from voting. Lord
Chancellor Richard West declared
in 1726, that 'the law does not
suppose any such person to exist as
an Irish Roman Catholic.' Fifty
years later, they owned only 5% of
the land of Ireland.

Edmund Burke (1722-97),
politician, writer and outstanding
rhetorician, whom Lord Lieutenant
Westmoreland (1790-95) accused
of being 'bent on inflammation'
(and whose statue stands inside the
front gate in Trinity College)
summarized the situation as follows:
'All the penal laws of that
unparalleled code of oppression
were manifestly the effects of
national hatred and scorn towards
a conquered people, whom the
victors delighted to trample upon
and were not at all afraid to provoke.
It was a machine of wise and
elaborate contrivance, as well fitted
for the oppression, impoverishment
and degradation of a people, and
the debasement in them of human
nature itself, as ever proceeded from
the perverted ingenuity of man'. [47]

JONATHAN SWIFT (1667-1745),
Anglican Dean of St Patrick's
Cathedral, author of *Gulliver's
Travels* and the foremost satirist ever
to write in the English language, was
born at No. 7 Hoey's Court,
immediately outside the Castle's
western curtain wall. He once had
rooms in the Castle, which he
almost destroyed by fire while
reading by candlelight. His
sculptured bust is above that of St.
Peter's at the entrance to the Chapel
Royal and he is also commemorated
by a plaque on the wall at the foot
of 'Castle Steps', Ship Street.

Swift reacted to the widespread
abject poverty and slum housing
conditions endured by the
downtrodden Catholics and the
Huguenot silk and woolen workers
unemployed because of England's

restrictive 'Irish Policy', in the once prosperous, industrialised, Liberties area that surrounded his Cathedral, by the use of his bitter penmanship. By means of his mostly anonymously published pamphlets, he proved to be a most able and spirited champion of the poor. His *Causes of the Wretched Condition of Ireland* lambasted 'the Egyptian bondage of cruel oppressing covetous landlords, expecting that all who live under them should make bricks without straw'. His best known historical pamphlet, *A Modest Proposal – for Preventing the Children of Poor People Becoming a Burden to their Parents or Country and for Making them Beneficial to the Public* (1729) attempted to arouse the social conscience of the English legislators: 'A young child is at a year old a most delicious, nourishing and wholesome food, whether stewed, roasted, baked or boiled.'

Nor was he averse to 'lashing out' at the Dublin Castle Court in general and the Lord Lieutenant (then commonly addressed as Viceroy) in particular. He declared publicly that Lord John Carteret, for whom 'life in Dublin was exile', was absent four fifths of the time Parliament sat during 1724. (They resided in the Castle only every second year from August to April – their second in command, such as the Lord Justice, governed in their

absence. From 1767, Viceroys were required to reside permanently in Ireland.) He was also the author of these forceful, hostile lines:

SO TO EFFECT HIS MONARCH'S ENDS
FROM HELL A VICEROY DEVIL ASCENDS
HIS BUDGET WITH CORRUPTIONS CRAMMED,
THE CONTRIBUTIONS OF THE DAMNED,
WHICH WITH UNSPARING HAND HE STREWS.

Swift suffered badly in his later years and predicted the loss of his mental faculties: "Like that tree, I shall die at the top." He affronted the Viceroy at a State banquet in the Castle by addressing him as: "You, fellow with the blue string." He experienced bouts of vertigo, nausea and melancholia (possibly Ménière's Syndrome or Alzheimer's Disease) and descended into insanity.

Throughout his life, he gave one third of his wealth to charity and in his will bequeathed funds for a new mental hospital (St. Patrick's). His tomb is in the nave of St. Patrick's Cathedral together with his death mask and pulpit. W.B. Yeats (Nobel Laureate) translated his Latin epitaph in *The Winding Stair*:

SWIFT HAS SAILED INTO HIS REST;
SAVAGE INDIGNATION THERE
CANNOT LACERATE HIS BREAST.
IMITATE HIM IF YOU DARE,
WORLD-BESOTTED TRAVELLER; HE
SERVED HUMAN LIBERTY.

The Growth of Dublin's Fair City

As late as the 1630s, Dublin was a medieval city with relatively limited international trading opportunities and its population of approximately 25,000 was still largely confined within the town walls.

The arrival of the Lord Deputy Thomas Wentworth (Earl of Stafford) in July 1633 coincided with a time of relative stability and heralded the commencement of economic growth and urban expansion. His inauguration ceremony commenced with the sword of State being carried in formal procession from the Earl of Corke's House to the new Gallery, where he awaited it. From thence he proceeded to the Presence Chamber (Throne Room) where he made 'two humble courtesies to the King's and Queen's picture (Charles 1 and Mary) and fixing his eyes with much seriousness, showed a kind of devotion'.

He described the Castle as being 'little better than a very prison' and proceeded to extend his living accommodation to 'make this habitation easeful and pleasant' for his family. A child of his was born and christened in the Castle in 1634 but died there aged two years. A visitor in 1635 praised the stately new stables that the Lord Deputy had provided for sixty horses, on land adjoining the eastern side of the Castle (on the site of the Treasury Block alongside the Poddle). The stalls were exceedingly high and no planks were used, 'but Holland bricks placed upon the edges, whereupon the horses lie and you walk'. He considered part of one of the towers to be in a dangerous condition and had it emolished and declared that others were 'so crazy as we are still in fear part of it might drop down upon our heads'. However, he regretted 'pulling down an old gate within the castle' as it supported a carved epigram honouring a former Viceroy: '... while time remains, praise for worthy Sidney will never end,' and had the block remounted over the new one.

Wentworth became one of the most energetic and efficient 'administrators and extractor of leases' ever to work in Dublin Castle and was worthy of his motto 'thorough'. Under his direction, the army was well disciplined, properly equipped and regularly paid, the Irish Sea was cleared of pirates (which had been a real and constant menace) and local industry, especially the linen business, was actively encouraged. An enthusiastic patron of the theatre, he stimulated the first professional performances in Dublin and frequently staged dramatic productions by the gentlemen of Court in the Great Hall. The Earl of Corke recorded that one such event had been really 'tragical, for we had no supper'.

An uncompromising and ostentatious politician, he regularly rode out on his black horse, clad in black armour with black plumes. It was not without reason that he was given the nickname 'Black Tom Tyrant' as, for example, he imprisoned Lord Chancellor Adam Loftus in 1638 for refusing to release lands at Monasterevin, Co. Kildare, to his son Robert (Loftus) to whom he (Wentworth) was related by marriage. The Chancellor petitioned King Charles for clemency, arguing that he was 'very aged and [the Castle] prison very close and pestered with prisoners', but, almost a year later, the strong willed King directed that he be kept in solitary confinement without access to visitors, until he agreed to release the land as directed.

The King had appointed Wentworth with instructions to end the corruption and wasteful extravagance of the Castle administration and to increase revenues to the monarchy. Although expenditure greatly exceeded his Lord Deputy's salary, he made a huge profit for himself and Charles by exploiting the rivalry between the New and Old English – which alienated all and made him many enemies. He assembled the Parliament in the Castle in 1641 and persuaded the members to allocate almost £250,000 for 'graces' – concessions that included guarantees against religious discrimination. Following receipt of the money, the King reneged on his promise, which incited many to join the rebellion of that year.

However, his desire to build a magnificent dream mansion for himself at Jigginstown (Naas, Co. Kildare) went badly wrong. It was rumoured that he imported so many red bricks that they were handed from person to person in a human chain that reached the 32km (20 miles) from Dublin Docks. Before its completion, he was recalled as chief Royal advisor in the growing crisis. A delegation of Old and New English travelled to London and testified at his impeachment tribunal that he was

justifiably hated. Abandoned by the King, he was hanged on the 12th May 1642 – a foreshadowing of the fate of his master.

Export trade continued to adapt and grow and became more market orientated – especially dairy produce for the European continent and woollen produce for the English market. However, the English 'Act For Encouragement of Trade' (1667) prohibited all exports of Irish cattle to England and ruined that business. Five years later, an Act prohibited the export of produce from the British colonies directly to Ireland. Smaller Irish ports suffered and some never recovered, but Dublin's trade grew through this process of centralised distribution and was now Ireland's principal port. Duties were imposed on Irish woollen exports in January 1699 and were extended two months later to prohibit woollen exports to any country other than England.

Large-scale deforestation opened up new tracts of land and agricultural systems and methods further improved. Not everybody was happy with these developments. An anonymous seventeenth century poet lamented the destruction of the forests in *Kilcash*:

CAD A DHEANFAIMID FEASTA GAN ADHMAD?

TÁ DEIREADH NA GCOILLTE AR LÁR.

(WHAT WILL WE DO FOR TIMBER?

THE LAST OF THE WOODS CUT DOWN.)

The appointment of James Butler, 1st Duke of Ormonde, as Lord Lieutenant in 1662 proved to be the greatest stimulus to Dublin's urban expansion. (He was the first Irish Chief Governor in more than a century and this, his second term, followed the restoration of the monarchy.) The population climbing steadily with former Cromwellian soldiers, Huguenot and other Protestant refugee families taking up permanent residence.

He issued an edict that thatched houses were to be re-roofed and that new houses were to be built of brick or stone with tile or slate roofs. He also actively encouraged development of the Grafton Street area (named after the Duke of Grafton, illegitimate son of the King Charles II) and St. Stephen's Green became a park 'set to the advantage of the city'. Humphrey Jervis, the developer, began construction of the north-side quays, including Ormond and Arran, and in 1676 erected Essex (now Grattan) Bridge to his new suburb of Capel Street (named after Lord Lieutenant Capel 1672-77). This was only two years after the construction of Dublin's second bridge at Watling Street, which was also known as Bloody Bridge on account of the ferrymen riot at its opening – four of whom were killed while under escort to the Castle's dungeons.

In 1663, a plot by some ex-Cromwellian adventurers to overpower the sentries at Ship Street Gate and capture the Castle was foiled when it was revealed to Ormonde. (They were aggrieved at being forced to relinquish some land grants to Catholic owners proved innocent of rebellion) Colonel Thomas Blood escaped but three co-conspirators, including the Member of Parliament for Trim, were hanged at Gallows Green, Parkgate Street. The postern gate in the western curtain wall was blocked up to improve security. Blood led an assassination attempt on Ormonde seven years later when, with a gang in the pay of a Parliamentary faction, they dragged him from his cab in a London street but, though 'fired upon, ridden over and struck with swords and pistols', Ormonde escaped. Blood was later pardoned for attempted theft of the English Crown Jewels and returned to Dublin as a Castle spy. [48]

The existence of Dublin's Phoenix Park (adapted from the Irish *fionn uisce* meaning white water) – the largest walled park in Europe, is one of his enduring legacies. King Charles 11 (son of Charles 1) had promised this land to his mistress, Lady Castlemaine, but was persuaded to change his mind and utilise it as a deer park instead. At their next social encounter, Lady Castlemaine 'fell upon Ormonde

below *'Ground Plott of the Castle', 1673 (simplified). Probably by William Robinson.*

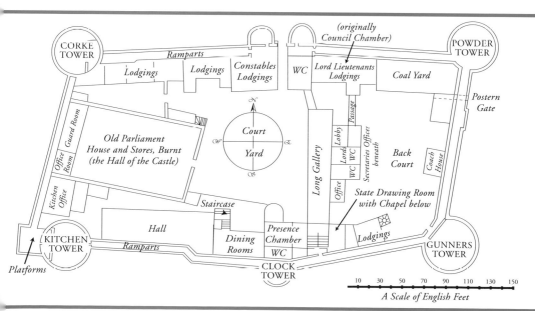

above Lord Lieutenant Ormonde in the robes of the Knights of the Garter.

with a torrent of abusive language' and told him that she hoped "to see him hanged" but received the reply that he "was not in so much haste to put an end to her days, for all he wished with regard to her was that he might live to see her old". (Lord Lieutenant Chesterfield introduced extensive planting, erected the Phoenix monument at his own expense and opened the park to the public in 1745.)

We are fortunate that a floor plan of the Castle in 1673 survives (see p.67) as it is our last view of it before the disastrous fire of 1684 changed everything. G.B. Maguire, in his article '17th Century Plans of Dublin Castle', coupled it with a detailed description of the old Castle in 1678 by Robert Ware – so making the picture complete.

The stately Long Gallery (1624) was 'born upon pillars in the nature of a piazza' and stretched almost the full (north/south) width of the courtyard, to a new grand entrance and staircase (on the same site as the present one) leading to the State Rooms, Chapel and Presence Chamber – where Ormonde had constructed the Battleaxe Hall. The 'Great Hall where the Courts of Justice and the Houses of Parliament used to sit, until the wisdom of the State thought fit to free the Castle from so great a concourse of people as usually frequented that great assembly', was raised on several elegant pillars. Gunpowder stored underneath was removed 'by God's admired providence' shortly before fire destroyed the building in 1671.

The Castle Gate Towers were used for 'the custody of his majesties [eminent] prisoners'. Immediately alongside were the Castle Constable's lodgings, which were 'very much beautified in Ormonde's time'. The Lord Lieutenant's Lodgings, which had been converted from Council Chambers, were on the other side of the gateway. (In his absence from Ireland, the next in command resided here.) The postern gate in the eastern curtain wall (beside the coal yard) had a permanent sentry on duty to supervise access to the stable yard – with its 'horse pond' where the Poddle broadened out in a hollow east of the stables, furniture store, mint and 'workhouse of armourers and smiths attached to the artillery train'.

Lord Deputy Richard Butler, Earl of Arran, (1682-84) sent a perfectly structured (and very suspicious) account of the GREAT FIRE of 1684 to his father the Duke of Ormonde, who was in London, within hours of the events that effectively ended Dublin Castle's function as a medieval fortress. According to it, the fire started between 1 am and 2 am on 7th April, on the wooden flooring under the fire grate in Arran's dressing room in his newly built lodgings. The crackling of the flames woke him and he fled through the State Rooms as far as the Long Gallery. There he stopped to look back and, as he had left all the intervening doors open, saw his bed on fire and the flames spreading quickly.

The sentries raised the alarm. Arran sent for Robert Cuffe, the Engineer – the Architect, William Robinson being out of town – who arrived shortly afterwards with six barrels of gunpowder from a private store. A controlled explosion at the southern end of the Long Gallery failed to halt the fire. So, another was set off at the northern end and this prevented it reaching the Lord Lieutenant's lodgings and the Powder Tower, via the coal yard. There was a westerly wind blowing

and a final explosion, near the Presence Chamber, succeeded in halting its advance along the southwest range to the Kitchen (Bermingham) Tower – which housed the public records.

Arran feared the rumours that might spread about the circumstances surrounding the fire and again wrote to his father on the 16th: 'I long to know how this matter is taken by His Majesty, and the Ministers of State, being, I think, justly afraid that in this malicious world, the thing may be so misrepresented as that I may be censured for what I could not help'.[49] The King issued a Royal warrant on 24th July, which declared that it had started accidentally and directed that the old walls and as many towers as required be taken down and a new Chief Governor's residence be built 'the same to be still and forever called by the name of the Castle of Dublin'. Henceforth it would be a

castle in name only. The age of fortified castles was over – gunpowder, mortars and large cannon having made them obsolete. Ormond returned to serve a third term of office and was replaced by Lord Lieutenant Clarendon in 1685.

John Dunton, a London bookseller, visited the Lower Castle Yard in 1698: 'Next to the chapel to which Lord Galway goes constantly every morning to prayers [and at his return spends some time in receiving petitions] is the office of the Ordnance near which the king's gunsmiths and armours work. Before these buildings lies a large piece of ground called the stable yard on the side of which are the king's stables… In this yard two companies of foot [soldiers] parade every morning, one which mounts the town guard and the other that of the Castle'. The River Poddle 'runs [northwards] here, on the other side of which stands the coach houses, and the biggest haystacks that I ever saw'.

At the rear of the State Apartments, he viewed a broad terrace walk 'the length of the building, the walls covered with greens and flower pots'. (This was removed in 1811 – in advance of the widening of the Back Avenue and construction of the gothic screen and terraced walls.) 'From hence on a stone arch over a little river you descend by two spacious pair of stone stairs into the garden, which is handsomely laid out into grass plots with green and gravel walks, and to the north side there are two rows of flourishing lime trees, beneath which lies another grass walk'.

Fast-growing Dublin was becoming a modern city. By the end of the century the population had doubled to 50,000, making it second in size and importance in the British Empire (and seventh in Europe). Large numbers of beggars and thieves, insufficient oil-fired public lighting (gaslight came in 1825) and rudimentary footpaths made walking unpleasant. Transportation was still largely undeveloped, but the narrow winding town streets were unable to cope with the increasing amounts of traffic and congestion was commonplace. [50] There was a fire brigade service – of which a water engine survives in St. Werburg's Church. Public hackney (taxi) coaches were regulated and assigned stands or ranks such as those in Werburg Street and Castle Street. The latter, leading to Castle Gate, was a main artery from Viking times to the opening of Lord Edward Street in 1886 and boasted a number of bookshops (such as the 'Stationer's Arms') and the first General Post Office.

Birth of Modern Dublin Castle

For much of the eighteenth century, Dublin thrived in a new era of peace and the population is estimated to have risen to 172,000 at the end of the century (and from 2 to $5^1/_4$ million nationally).

The market and working-class areas remained to the west and north west of town, where streets were narrow and alleyways were crowded with shops and small industries. This was also the case in the town centre, which still possessed the medieval street pattern (although it had long since burst through its medieval walls).

A marked east-west social and economic divide had developed, however, as the powerful and wealthy moved their households eastwards. The newly constructed elegantly uniform squares of St. Stephen's Green, Fitzwilliam and Merrion (named after the developer Viscount Fitzwilliam of Merrion) attracted the 'nobility, gentry and the liberal professions'. North of the Liffey, the extended and commercialised Sackville Street (after Lord Lieutenant Sackville 1730-32 and 1750-52 and reopened by the Wide Street Commission in 1784) was home to 'persons of the first rank and opulence'. Rutland Square, (after the Lord Lieutenant 1784-87 and renamed after the nationalist leader, Charles Stewart Parnell) and Mountjoy Square

below The Castle from Charles Brooking's map of Dublin, 1728.

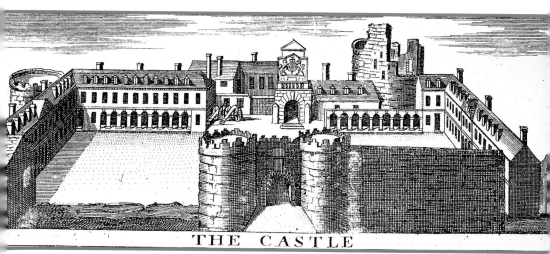

THE CASTLE

(named after Luke Gardiner, Viscount Mountjoy) were inhabited principally by 'the mercantile and official class', while the adjacent Rotunda Gardens became a fashionable promenade ground.

This was also the time when Dublin Castle and the surrounding streets took on their modern form. The illustration from Brooking's map (p.71) shows the Castle as it was in 1728, during its transition years. (Orientation is southwards and the descriptions follow it in a clockwise direction.) Castle Gate Towers, Record Tower, the Apartments (entrance, great staircase, dining room and old hall), the semi dilapidated Bermingham Tower (where the lower floors continued in use) and the north-west curtain wall are still in existence. However, the main elements of Robinson's master plan (which took sixty years to complete) were well underway.

The north-east curtain wall was demolished, while the adjacent east cross block has been completed, with the Office of the Chief Secretary in the northern half. (This post originated as personal secretary to the Lord Lieutenant in the previous century and this accommodation later became the annex to his new office.) The Privy Council chamber was sited in the centre under the (triangular) pediment – where the War Office had been located in former times.

The Lord Lieutenants were 'sworn in' here and their Offices were accommodated in the southern half of the block. The adjoining south-east range was also finished and housed the principal State drawing rooms and bedrooms. The corresponding south-west and west ranges were, likewise, completed with attic storeys lit by dormer windows. The ground floor open arcades (1726) were used as parking spaces for sedan chairs (some of which had cupolas to accommodate elaborate hairpieces) while their owners or hirers attended Castle Court functions.

By 1720, building works had been finished in the east building for the Trustees of the Linen, and the new Treasury block (on the site formerly occupied by Wentworth's stables) in the Lower Castle Yard – a general location that habitually referred to everything not in the Upper Castle Yard. Today, the Comptroller and Auditor General's Office occupies the latter, which is the oldest dedicated office block in Dublin (see photo opposite and bird's-eye view inside front cover).

King George II issued a royal warrant in 1737, for the demolition of 'the Great Staircase, Battleaxe Hall, Chaplain's Apartments and the Castle entrance – being in most ruinous condition'. The north-east block was completed within the following ten years and became the

above *The Treasury Building, constructed 1717, Lower Castle Yard.*

Chief Secretary's Office (to which a northern extension was added in the 1790s on the former Horse Guard Yard).

Philip Dormer Stanhope was appointed Lord Lieutenant Chesterfield in 1745 and found that the King's instructions had yet to be implemented and that his apartments were 'not only in the most ruinous condition, but in immediate danger of falling to the ground although continually propped'. He initiated the construction of the State Apartments and by 1761, the main rooms were completed – including the present grand entrance, which was open to the courtyard until the 1820's; the Battleaxe staircase, roughly on the site of the old; a new suite of bedrooms; the State Corridor; the Throne Room; the Picture Gallery, originally a supper room; and the ballroom, now St Patrick's Hall (where a bronze bust of Chesterfield, by Roubilac, is on display). [51]

The Army's Ordnance Department managed the country's central munitions depot in the Castle. Artillery was sited in the Upper Castle Yard and in the Artillery Ground (beside the Armoury, east of the garden – see map p.94) until the construction of Islandbridge Barracks in 1797.

above *The Great Courtyard (or Upper Castle Yard) in 1792, by James Malton. The State Apartments are to left and Bedford Tower to right. (The tower of St. Werburgs, in the far background, was later removed for security reasons)*

(This was formerly known as the Gun Carriage Yard and became the Police Barrack's Yard in 1838.) Gunpowder, originally stored in the Towers and on the ground floor of the old Parliament House, had been moved into the powder house in the gardens. This exploded in 1689 and consequently, a large magazine was built in the Phoenix Park (1732). A new Castle munitions store, workshop and laboratory was then constructed near Ship Street Gate. However, it too blew up (1764) damaging houses in Ship Street, the roof of the Ballroom and the remaining superstructure of the Bermingham Tower – which was taken down to first-floor level and rebuilt (1777). [52] The Ordnance Office was built on this (munitions store) site in 1820.

The Wide Street Commission was a development agency set up by Act of Parliament in 1757 and given extensive powers for the widening of streets, including compulsory purchase of properties, regulation of building standards and, at a later stage, control of town planning. (Their functions were later assumed by the Corporation.) They held their early meetings in the Castle, where they concentrated initially on improving its approach roads.

An Act was passed the following year 'to make a wide and convenient street from Essex Bridge to the Royal Castle of Dublin'. (The bridge was rebuilt in 1775 and was fitted with public lighting (1779) as it was 'subject to many mischiefs at night'.) Bise's Tower was demolished, because it stood in the middle of the proposed street, and 'offending' properties were purchased along the planned route. When the residents changed their minds about selling, the Wide Street Commissioners 'unroofed the houses in the middle of the night to get people out for the street widening'. Parliament Street was opened in 1762.

Plans had been made for the construction of a much wider main entrance to the Castle, in line with Cork Hill, which necessitated demolition of all the houses from 'Doran the Joiner' to the site of the old Castle Gate – which had been demolished in 1750. The appropriate properties were compulsorily purchased. However, the Commissioners failed with their scheme to turn the adjoining site into an open space to enhance the new Cork Hill entrance. An article in Faulkner's Journal of 12th July 1768 stated that 'the workmen began to throw down the old buildings of Cork Hill, in order to widen the avenue and prepare the ground for erecting the new Royal Exchange, or Merchants' Business Centre, at Cork Hill'. Lord Lieutenant Townsend laid the foundation stone of what is now City Hall the following year. (In 1785, Dame [formerly Dam] Street,

which had been narrow and very crowded – especially during parliamentary sittings, was upgraded 'to open a convenient street, from his Majesty's Castle of Dublin to the Parliament'.)

A new gateway was erected from the Lower Castle Yard, where Castle Lane had been widened and renamed Palace Street. Ground was purchased on Cork Hill, north of the old Castle Gate site, and the new Guard House and Court Martial Room (the façade of which bounds modern Castle Hall) were

below The dramatic spiral staircase of Bedford Tower.

constructed inside the new grand Cork Hill entrance. These works and the north-west range was finished by 1758.

Bedford Tower was completed in 1761, during the term of Lord Lieutenant Bedford, and became the centrepiece of the 'new look' Upper Castle Yard. Its rusticated arches support ionic columns and pediment from which rise a circular Corinthian lantern and cupola. The balcony was used by State musicians, who gained access via the interior cantilever stairway. It was first occupied by the Dean of the Chapel Royal, then housed the offices of the Second Secretary, subsequently the Master of Ceremonies and the Viceroy's aide-de-camps and later still the Office of Arms. (It now forms part of the Castle's conference facilities and an original marble dial is displayed in Castle Hall.)

Bedford Tower was flanked by two massive inner arches (1751) – their heavy broken pediments supporting the lead sculptures of Justice and Fortitude by Van Nost the Younger (1753) – in which the Castle authorities, already sensitive to the criticism that Justice had its back turned to the city, bored holes to restore equilibrium to her tilting scales.

The completed Upper Castle Yard represented the last appearance of brick on the grand scale. 'The total effect, in red brick with cream stone trimmings, segment-headed ground-floor windows and arcades at salient points, is charming in an intimate collegiate fashion, persuading one to forget the evil role of the Castle in Irish affairs.' [53] It is acknowledged that the north side of the courtyard presents one of the most beautiful architectural compositions in Dublin – 'reflecting the serene architecture of the Renaissance'. The gate of Justice now provides the emblem of the Revenue Commissioners and Bedford Tower is the symbol and logo of the modern Dublin Castle facilities.

The Illustrious Order of St. Patrick and Theft of the Irish Crown Jewels

above *Installation Dinner of the Knights of St. Patrick, St. Patrick's Hall, 17th March 1785.*

The Great Hall, or ballroom, became known as St Patrick's Hall when the Knights of the most 'Illustrious Order of St Patrick' were first invested there, in 1783, by Lord Lieutenant George Nugent Grenville Temple, under warrant of King George III. The central panel of Waldé's cciling paintings, which was commissioned by Viceroy Temple in 1787 during his second term of office, represents the establishment of the chivalric Order in allegorical form, with the King seated between the symbolic figures of Great Britain (with flag) and Ireland (with harp) accompanied by Liberty and Justice, with Fame blowing her trumpet while cherubs hold the crown, sword and blue hat of the institution (see photo p.137).

This was the Irish equivalent of the English Orders of the Garter and the Bath and the Scottish Order of the Thistle. It consisted of the Monarch, a Grand Master – the Viceroy, and twenty-two knights who were usually supporters of the government or those whose support was required. Earl Temple was well pleased that his hard work had born fruit and notified his brother that 'our Order is wonderfully popular' and that 'half Dublin is mad about the Order'.

Their king-size, eight-pointed, star is sited above the east doorway and a gold ceremonial knight's badge, with each leaf of shamrock terminating in a Royal crown and superimposed on the cross of St. Patrick (signifying the close union between Ireland and Britain), is on view at the north wall. The wall mounted stall plates chronologically record the names and the banners bear the family crests of the knights invested between 1871-1922.

In addition to administrating the protocol and precedence at Dublin Castle Court, the Office of Arms (established 1552) was the registry of the Order – where certificates of nobility were endorsed and family histories and noteworthy achievements of these Irish peers were catalogued. The royally appointed Ulster King of Arms (Chief Herald of Ireland) was the Knight Attendant and Registrar of the Order. During the early-nineteenth century he was described as 'the first and only permanent officer of the Lord Lieutenant's household with full responsibility for arranging all the public ceremonies connected with Government – such as the proclamation of a new sovereign or peace or war, the reception and inauguration of the Lord Lieutenant, custody of all records respecting such matters and keeping a record of all State proceedings'.[54]

The orders insignia, or regalia, which became known as the Irish Crown Jewels, had been awarded by King George IV in 1830 and consisted of a Grand Master's

above Grand Master Arthur Vicars, in ceremonial dress.

Diamond Star, which, according to the Dublin Metropolitan Police reward notice (see photo) was $4^1/_2$ x $4^1/_2$ inches [11.4cm] and contained '150 white, pure, Brazilian diamonds issuing from the centre, enclosing a cross of rubies and a shamrock of emeralds.' The Grand Master's Diamond Badge was '3 x $2^1/_2$ inches [7.6 x 6.3 cm] 'set in silver, with a shamrock of emeralds on a ruby cross, surrounded by a sky blue enamelled circle – with their motto: *Quis Seperabit* MDCCLXXXIII [who shall separate it, 1783] in rose diamonds, surrounded by a wreath of shamrocks – the whole surmounted by a circle of large single Brazilian stones, surmounted by a crowned harp in diamonds.'

Prior to 1903, they were stored in a bank vault when not in use. Then they were transferred to a steel safe, which was to be placed in the newly constructed strong room in the Bedford Tower. However, the safe proved to be too large for the doorway. Arthur Vicars, the Ulster King of Arms, who had been knighted by Viceroy Cadogan in 1896 and made Commander of the Victorian Order by King Edward VII (son of Queen Victoria) in 1901, was responsible for the safekeeping of the jewels by letters patent (under seal of state). He had diligently supervised the recent

above DMP reward notice of 10th July 1907, issued by the Detective Department, Exchange Court.

move of the Office from the Record Tower and now agreed to them being stored in the safe in the ground floor public office and library instead – as he believed the location (adjacent to the Castle sentries and Guard House) to be secure.

On Saturday morning, 6th July 1907, just four days before the State visit of King Edward and Queen Alexandra, it was discovered that they had been stolen – following a number of successively more obvious clues left by the thief or thieves, including the front door of the building and strong room being left unlocked. There was no sign of illegal entry and the newspaper reports were accurate in their assertions that 'the safe had been opened in a regular manner and how anyone could, unobserved, burglariously enter the Office of Arms…passes all ordinary comprehension' [55] as the location was 'at all hours of the twenty-four, constantly and systematically occupied by soldiers and policemen.'[56] Neither the jewels nor Vicars' mother's jewellery, which he also kept in the cabinet, were located, despite extraordinary efforts – including his attendance at a séance and subsequent fruitless searches of graveyards in north Co. Dublin.

The Royal visit had been meticulously planned, with the investiture of a knight in St. Patrick's Hall featuring prominently. The theft was given abundant coverage by the press and diverted public interest from the programme – which infuriated the King, who cancelled the ceremony and instructed Viceroy Aberdeen to dismiss Vicars from office. Aberdeen offered him a pension to resign, but Vicars refused to do so, although under great pressure – including the deliberate leaking of lurid stories about his alleged homosexuality (which was then a criminal offence) and rumours of regular 'wild parties' in the Office of Arms.

Vicars demanded a public inquiry, but a private Viceregal Commission was established instead, which he refused to attend. Furthermore, he accused Frances Shackleton, Dublin Herald and his second in command (who was also his co-tenant and a brother of Ernest, the Antarctic explorer) of involvement in the theft.

The three Commissioners excluded the press and sat for six days in the same public office where the theft had taken place. Their terms of reference limited the investigation to ascertaining who was responsible for their custody, but in the acquittal of Shackleton – a prime suspect who had predicted the theft, had access to the keys and was seriously in debt – they exceeded their limits of responsibility by stating categorically that he was found to be 'entirely innocent'. (Four years later, he was jailed for fifteen months for misappropriating a widow's savings.) Vicars, being the custodian of the jewels, was found guilty and sacked.

He spent his remaining years in a 'big house' in Co. Kerry, where his support of the local Royal Irish Constabulary during the War of Independence led to his death. On 14th April 1921, an IRA contingent took him out of blazing Kilmorna Castle, shot him dead and hung a message around his neck which claimed that he was an informer.

Vicars had always believed that he had taken the blame for the failings of others and had been treated 'outrageously' by the Castle and his King. In his will he recorded: 'I am unconscious of having done anything wrong and my misfortune arose from being unsuspicious and trusting a one time friend.'

There are many theories about the robbery and the culprits. Lord Haddo, the eldest son of Viceroy Aberdeen, was seen in the Office of Arms shortly before the theft and had previously taken the jewels as a practical joke, during one of Vicars' soirées. Shackleton, with the aid of an associate, had motive and opportunity and was the chief suspect of Inspector Kane of Scotland Yard, yet King Edward protected him – presumably because of the threat of publicising his intimate relationship with the King's brother-in-law. [57]

A further plausible explanation, though lacking in evidence, claims that Owen Kerr, a Dublin Metropolitan Policeman, stole the jewels on his normal security circuit, as part of a Unionist conspiracy to publicise the extensive homosexual network in the Castle (which included Shackleton and Haddo) on the eve of the Royal visit and so force the resignation of the 'Home Rule' Viceroy Aberdeen and through him, fatally damage that faction in the British Liberal Party. [58]

Whatever the truth of the matter, the King ordered the purging of this 'shocking, lurid and sensational' scandal and so it was completely suppressed and the career of an innocent man was ruined. All papers relating to the theft, including those of the DMP, Scotland Yard, the King (who died three years later), the Office of Arms 'Letter Book' for the period and the documentary evidence, were destroyed.

Viceroy Aberdeen continued his second term in office (1905-1915) – the longest since the Act of Union (see also p. 104). As Ireland is a Republic, this Order of Knighthood is no longer in existence. The Chief Herald of Ireland and Genealogical Office are now in Kildare Street. The mystery of the missing Irish Crown Jewels has never been solved.

above Official portrait of John Gordon Campbell – Lord Lieutenant Aberdeen, 1913. He is shown holding the sword of State and wearing the collar, star and badge of the Order of the Thistle.

The 1798 Rebellion

Europe and the Americas exploded into revolution in the closing decades of the eighteenth century and many liberal English statesmen sympathised with the many laudable social, economic and national causes – provided they took place overseas and 'not in their back yard'.

As only landowning Anglican males could vote, the creation of a secular republic based on *liberté, égalité, fraternité* became the ideal of new revolutionary groups such as the United Irishmen. They were founded in Belfast, in 1791, by disillusioned members of the Protestant ascendancy, with the intention of advancing human-rights issues including equality for Catholics, and formed a loose (and not always harmonious) alliance with The Defenders – a Catholic secret society. Even constitutional nationalists had become radicalised, as the government refused to concede adequate reforms.

The Castle administration was well aware that the United Irishmen were in direct communication with the revolutionary French Government (which was now at war with Britain) and the Irish Parliament passed harsh new laws – including an Arms Act, a Gunpowder Act and an Insurrection Act – which allowed Lord Lieutenant Camden (1795-98) impose curfews and place any 'disturbed' district under martial law. Alarmingly, the spectre of French invasion loomed large as Wolfe Tone, the founding father of the United Irishmen and modern Irish republicanism, persuaded the French Directory to send an invasion fleet of forty-eight ships and 14,500 soldiers in 1776, to support an insurrection and so liberate Ireland and create a Republic:

OH THE FRENCH ARE IN THE BAY
THEY'LL BE HERE WITHOUT DELAY
AND THE ORANGE WILL DECAY
SAYS THE SEAN BEAN BOCHT

(Traditional ballad: *Sean Bean Bocht* = Poor Old Woman, meaning Ireland.)

The fleet was prevented from landing at Bantry Bay by bad weather, but its arrival raised morale and membership of the United Irishmen. A full-time Irish Militia had been established three years earlier and Crown forces were now further strengthened by the formation of the Irish Yeomanry, which were recruited and commanded by the gentry, and the deployment of large-scale reinforcements in 1797, which brought total troop numbers to over 30,000. The Lord Lieutenant ordered disarming of the rebels by whatever means considered necessary. A reign of terror ensued with killings, half hangings, pitch-cappings and house burnings becoming daily occurrences, while the Castle authorities ignored complaints of abuse. However, 'flogging rebellion out of the radicals' only drove others to insurrection and eventually, the Great Rebellion of 1798 erupted in a number of counties – most notably in Wexford, Carlow, Kildare, Meath, Down, and Antrim.

Dublin too was preparing for the rising and weapons were distributed among the greatly increased numbers of United Irishmen. Their strategy included the capture of significant buildings such as Parliament House and Trinity College. The northside men of Santry planned to assault the Infantry Barracks (in a row of houses) in South Great Georges Street, immediately outside the Castle's eastern perimeter, while a squad from the southside seized the Upper Castle Yard in a surprise attack.

However, Under Secretary Edward Cooke efficiently administered a very effective network of spies and informers from a generous secret service fund, and learnt of most plans in advance of implementation. For example, the United Irishmen's defence counsel, Leonard McNally, was a double agent and the spymaster Francis Higgins directed ten agents and regularly reported 'findings' to Cooke in person. [59] Higgins was responsible for the capture of many rebel leaders including the Commander in Chief of the United Irishmen, Lord Edward Fitzgerald, who was fatally injured by Major Henry Sirr, Chief of Police, in Thomas Street on 19th May. Two days later, Dublin town was placed under martial law, with a strict 9 pm to 5 am curfew.

Despite these serious setbacks, orders were issued for the rising to commence in Dublin at 10 pm on Wednesday 23rd. Informants promptly delivered this crucial information to Cooke and 'all was lost'. Extensive weapons searches and large-scale arrests were made and massed ranks of local well-armed yeomanry and government troops blockaded the Liffey bridges and the town's main approach roads – so preventing reinforcement by the rebel forces that encircled the town for a week. According to the loyalist parlia-mentarian, Baron Richard Musgrave: 'If they had preceded us by ever so small a space of time, the fate of the city and its loyal inhabitants would have been decided. For the mass of the people, armed with pikes and other weapons, were lurking in lanes, alleys and bye-ways, ready to start forth on the first beat of their drums and would have occupied all the streets and assassinated the yeomen before they could have reached their respective stations.'

Many rebels were hung from Carlisle (O'Connell) and other bridges and from gallows in army barracks throughout Dublin, as a terrible warning to others. The Royal Exchange (City Hall) was converted into a military depot in which courts martial were held and 'torture was inflicted here and the screams of the sufferers might have been audible in the very offices where the Ministers of the government met to perform their functions' [60]

Sir Jonah Barrington, lawyer and Member of Parliament, gave the following account of events that took place in the Castle on May 25th, following a cavalry charge that had dispersed the Santry men: 'Some dead bodies of insurgents, sabred the night before by Lord Roden's dragoons, were brought in a cart to Dublin, with some prisoners tied together: the carcasses were stretched out in the [Upper] Castle Yard, where the Viceroy then resided, and in full view of the Secretary's windows: they lay on the pavement as trophies of the first skirmish, during a hot day, cut and gashed in every part, covered with clotted blood and dust, the most frightful spectacle which ever disgraced a royal residence save the seraglio.

After several hours exposure, some appearance of life was perceived in one of the mutilated carcasses. The man had been stabbed and gashed in various parts; his body was removed to the guard room and means were taken to restore animation; the efforts succeeded, he entirely recovered and was pardoned by Lord Camden. He was an extraordinarily fine young man, above 6ft [1.8m] high, the son of a Mr Keogh, an opulent landholder of Rathfarnham; he did not, however, change his principles and was, ultimately, sent out of the country.'[61]

The rising in the capital, which was the cause of the Castle's greatest anxiety, had been crushed before it began and the town was derided as 'the dog that didn't even bark'. Many Dubliners, including weavers from the Liberties, joined the struggle elsewhere and became fugitive rebels, while some did so on a part-time basis especially, according to Musgrave, 'when the rebels were about to make any great effort in Wexford, Wicklow or Kildare.' 'Safe houses' in the town and county harboured some of the wounded and weapons continued to be smuggled from town to the rebel armies. Women were particularly active in this and in recruitment, administering oaths, intelligence gathering and as confidential couriers.

The rebel leaders often wore their hair long but the foot soldiers, or 'croppies', shaved their heads so as not to get entangled in their three-pronged pike – one of which was used to cut horses reins, another to dismount the rider and the spear tip to skewer him. Their staple food on the march was grain, which sprouted where it fell. Hundreds are believed to be buried in Croppies' Acre, behind the 1798 memorial on Wolfe Tone Quay. Seamus Heaney, the Nobel Laureate, remembered them:[62]

Cooke wrote to Westminster in July (a few weeks after the fateful Battle of Vinegar Hill) with utmost satisfaction: 'Dublin and the county of Dublin are quiet.' The following month, a small French expeditionary force of 1,000 men landed on the west coast but it was too little, too late and was defeated. They were treated as prisioners of war, but 2,000 of their Irish allies were massacred – bringing the estimated total number of deaths to over 30,000. Ironically the Rebellion, which had been fought to break the connection with Britain, brought about the Act of Union instead. (However, the desire for an Irish Republic wasn't extinguished.)

Requiem for the Croppies

THE POCKETS OF OUR GREATCOATS FULL OF BARLEY –

NO KITCHENS ON THE RUN, NO STRIKING CAMP –

WE MOVED QUICK AND SUDDEN IN OUR OWN COUNTRY.

THE PRIEST LAY BEHIND DITCHES WITH THE TRAMP.

A PEOPLE, HARDLY MARCHING – ON THE HIKE –

WE FOUND TACTICS HAPPENING EACH DAY:

WE'D CUT THROUGH REINS AND RIDER WITH THE PIKE

AND STAMPEDE CATTLE INTO INFANTRY,

THEN RETREAT THROUGH HEDGES WHERE CAVALRY MUST BE THROWN.

UNTIL, ON VINEGAR HILL, THE FATAL CONCLAVE.

TERRACED THOUSANDS DIED, SHAKING SCYTHES AT CANNON.

THE HILLSIDE BLUSHED, SOAKED IN OUR BROKEN WAVE.

THEY BURIED US WITHOUT SHROUD OR COFFIN

AND IN AUGUST THE BARLEY GREW UP OUT OF THE GRAVE.

above Romantic image published to commemorate the centenary of the Rebellion.

Its near success persuaded the government forces of the urgency of regaining effective control. Reprisals and repression were swift and ferocious. Lord Lieutenant Cornwallis (1798-1801), who had surrendered to George Washington at the decisive Battle of Yorktown in 1781 and later became Governor-General of India) was the Commander in Chief of the army who directed the vigorous suppression of the rebellion. Afterwards, he adopted a more conciliatory approach, and tried to curb some of the worst excesses of his forces. He offered a general amnesty – provided the insurgents surrendered all weapons, and also personally inspected and moderated many courts martial verdicts.

Approximately 700 political prisoners were hanged and 775 were transported to Botany Bay, where some were freed (but not allowed return) as their non jury trial proceedings hadn't been recorded and their crimes weren't known to the authorities. Most remained and made a new life for themselves in Australia. One such was Michael Dwyer, who arrived on board the *Tellicherry* following a voyage of over 160 days, and became High Commissioner of Sydney in 1815.

The final act of revolution was delivered in 1803 by Robert Emmet, United Irishman and son of the State Physician to the Viceroy. His family lived in the, extant, Sick and Indigent Room Keepers' Society building immediately outside the Castle's Palace Street Gate (which had previously been the home of Sirr). He had been a confidential messenger in 1798 and, on returning from a failed mission to secure French military aid, set about recruiting insurgents and stockpiling weapons including gunpowder, grenades and pikes.

His planning for rebellion was detailed and precise, as was his targeting of a number of significant

below Robert Emmet's execution scene outside St. Catherine's Church, Thomas Street.

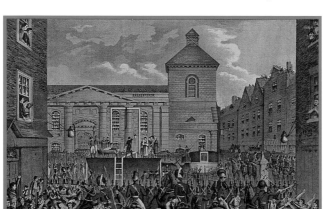

above The Castle (or Forty) Steps connect Ship Street Gate to Castle Street. (1930s photograph).

leaders and strategic sites and constituted a real threat to the Castle authorities – particularly in view of the resumption of war between Britain and France. However, his policy that only a core group would know when and where it would occur was self defeating in that not only did Castle informers not receive accurate information but neither did many potential insurgents.

An explosion in an arms depot in Patrick Street forced him to advance his plans and the insurrection began at 9 pm on Saturday 23rd July. He had overestimated his capability as a motivator and many who had gathered viewed him and the situation, balanced the inevitable fierce reprisals against their slight chance of success, and left. Emmet led less than 200 men from Marshalsea Lane (off Thomas Street) on an attack on the now only target of Dublin Castle (2km eastwards),

but also proved to be an ineffective military leader in combat as they never got that far because, at Vicar Street, they met the progressive Chief Justice Kilwarden fleeing his home at Newlands Cross for the safety of his town house in Leinster Street. The mob dragged him and his nephew from the carriage and piked them to death, and his daughter raised the alarm. Emmet then acknowledged that they weren't competent enough to achieve their goal and abandoned the rising.

He remained in Dublin because of his love for a woman and was arrested and detained in the Record Tower – where he was interrogated in the presence of Chief Secretary Wickham and Under Secretary Marsden on 30th August. He stood throughout his twelve-hour trial, during which he derided the 'irritable, harassing' Judge: that "Lord Norbury might easily drown in the blood of those he had sent to the gallows". Then, in his extraordinary oration from the dock, he called for a continuance of "this struggle of the oppressed against the oppressor" and handed on the 'flaming torch of rebellion' to future generations.

Emmet was hung, drawn, quartered and beheaded that same day (20th September, see opposite) and his body was concealed. Twenty-one of his comrades were also executed, and there are commemorative plaques to them at St. Catherine's Church. The dining table of Lord Norbury, who was Chief Justice from 1800-27, is on view in the King's Bedroom, State Apartments.

This rebellion once again highlighted the Castle's vulnerability and made security a pressing issue. The internal route from Palace Street to Ship Street was closed to the public and the stone bridge, which linked the State Apartments to the garden, was removed. (The present one dates from the 1820s.) The houses off Cole Alley, which adjoined the western perimeter – where the old curtain walls had been demolished almost fifty years

previously, were compulsorily purchased and pulled down. (Emmet had intended to penetrate the Castle via these houses.) The present Ship Street Gate, Guard House and high perimeter wall with return along Castle Street were constructed, while the new Castle Steps (on the site of Cole Alley) facilitated easy access to Castle Street and Castle Gate (see photo p.87 and rampart in photo on back cover). Later, the tower of St. Werburg's church was removed, as it provided a vantage point for sniper fire into the Upper Castle Yard.

Houses and shops on the east side of Great Ship Street, some of which bordered the Ordnance stores, were also acquired and some were demolished. In 1805, the buildings that became known as Ship Street Blocks A to F were converted into accommodation for the Ordnance Office of the Royal Engineers (which was abolished in 1855). Block M was constructed in 1811 beside Ship Street Gate, on the site of the former Provost Marshal's Prison, to house the Quartermaster General. A new central gatehouse (Blocks I and J – c 1860) protruded to allow line of fire along the full length of Great Ship Street. With the adjacent buildings, it became part of the new Ship Street Infantry Barracks.

left Ship Street Barracks buildings.

The Castle in the Aftermath of the Union

Following the political instability that accompanied the 1798 rebellion, Prime Minister Pitt was determined to extinguish the 'ascendancy' Irish Parliament and transfer its legislative powers to Westminster. Lord Lieutenant Cornwallis, in tandem with Chief Secretary Castlereagh, successfully steered the Act of Union through the Irish Parliament, which met for the last time on 2nd August 1800. A number of politicians were awarded peerages, patronage and 'disturbance monies' (bribery) were distributed generously and after 500 years in being, it voted itself out of existence.

The United Kingdom of Great Britain and Ireland was established on 1st January 1801 and the new united imperial flag – the Union Jack incorporating the flag of St. Patrick – was flown over Bedford Tower. The brass chandeliers with interwoven shamrocks (which symbolise Ireland) roses (England) and thistles (Scotland) of the Throne Room and Bermingham Tower Room commemorate this event.

Cornwallis resigned the following month (and again became Governor-General of India) as King George III vetoed Parliament's further consideration of Catholic emancipation – the stress of which he believed to be responsible for his later bout of insanity. Many Catholics had welcomed the Union on the understanding that freedom from legal, judicial and political inequalities would follow, and their continued exclusion prevented any possible growth in public popularity for the Castle. Policy was now determined at Westminster (where Ireland was under - represented by 100 Members of Parliament and four Anglican Bishops – with four peers in the House of Lords). An Irish Office was established to facilitate communication with the Castle authorities.

The Chief Secretary's Office continued to manage the day to day government of Ireland, under the direction of the Viceroy, who was usually a nobleman by birth; the Chief Secretary, often a young politician with ambition and stamina for this very demanding job; and the Under Secretary, a Civil Servant familiar with the Irish scene. These collectively were the Chief Executive Officers of the Irish Executive – also known as the Irish government. The Viceroy, Chief Secretary, Attorney General, Solicitor General and Lord

Chancellor were substituted with each change of government.

Initially the relationship between Lord Lieutenant and Chief Secretary remained unchanged with the Chief Secretary reporting directly to him. Robert Peel, Chief Secretary (1812-18) and future Prime Minister, recorded that he 'could do no act whatever independent of the authority of Viceroy Richmond' (1807-13). However, the situation reversed permanently with the appointment of Lord Lieutenant Whitworth (1813-17). Peel exercised his experience and capability to confine his authority to that of representing the King at social functions; holding court in the Castle; granting pardons; drafting pension lists; making regular donations to the 'loyal press' and distributing significant patronage – including appointments of local sheriffs, the judiciary and certain positions in the Army and Civil Service.

In 1830, the post of Chief Secretary was elevated to Cabinet level – where most policy was formulated – so making it an extremely powerful position. He now developed legislation, directed the police forces and the administration of services throughout Ireland, and had eleven departments under his control. Most of the twenty-four government departments, which were located

within or in close proximity to the Castle, conducted their business with the Irish Executive through his Office's three major divisions: Finance (which reviewed and forwarded estimates to London), Administration, and Judicial. [63]

The post of Lord Lieutenant now lacked real power in the Castle administration and degenerated to that of figurehead with only the appearance of power. The numbers of his household, most of whom were 'squeezed, sorely cribbed and cabined into little sets of rooms', was now the measure of his importance. Not un-typically, they included two private secretaries, an assistant private secretary, comptroller, chaplain, gentleman usher, usher-at-large and at-waiting, chamberlain, master of the horse, master and composer of the music, three aides, physician, surgeon oculist and dentist in ordinary and to the household – 'these last being entitled to appear at the levées'. His bodyguards, the Battleaxe Guards – which were similar to the 'Beefeaters' at the Tower of London, were disbanded in 1831 on economic grounds and replaced with regular troops.

The former head ranger's house in the Phoenix Park was renovated and greatly extended, and became the Viceregal Lodge. In 1833, Lord Lieutenant Wellesley (1821-28 and 1833-34, the eldest brother of

Wellington – 'The Iron Duke') moved his household into what is now the Irish President's official residence of *Áras an Uachtaráin*. The Chief Secretary and Under Secretary were also provided with attractive houses nearby.

The Act of Union greatly reduced Dublin's status to that of provincial city and it also declined in commercial and manufacturing importance as her unprepared small industries faced overwhelming competition from large scale, mass produced English products. Social deprivation, which had been commonplace before the Act of Union, increased unchecked.

There was a mass exodus of the resident nobility and gentry their dependants to London. Many left their grand houses to be managed by agents who converted some into multiple single-room dwellings at increasingly exorbitant weekly rack rents. This happened particularly in the former Gardiner estates (see p.72) where property values crashed – with the market price of one building falling from £8,000 in 1791 to £500 in the 1840s. Urban decay spread house by house, block by block and street by street, as formerly fashionable terraces deteriorated into tenements and slums.[64] The British army offered the only work opportunity for many men and the money sent home from foreign postings, 'put food on the family table.'

below Bringing in the prisoners following the short-lived Fenian Rising. From the Illustrated London News, 16th March 1867.

above *Dublin Metropolitan Police, in front of the Coach House.*

The situation hadn't improved much by the end of the century. A report on public health in Dublin in 1894 affirmed that the high death rate was due to grinding poverty and revealed that one third of the inhabitants lived in single rooms of 6,196 buildings – many condemned by the Corporation as 'unfit for human habitation' – in which they ate, cooked, slept and often carried on their employment. (The last tenements were pulled down in the 1940s.) [65]

The Constabulary of Ireland Act of 1836 empowered Under Secretary Thomas Drummond (1835-40) to amalgamate the rural Constabulary and the Peace Preservation Force (which had been formed by Peel to subdue 'disturbed' areas) into a new armed rural Irish Constabulary in order to tackle 'agrarian unrest and agitation', under the centralised command of an Inspector General. The Treasury Building in the Lower Castle Yard was substantially repaired and the western half served as his Constabulary Office. Queen Victoria renamed it the Royal Irish Constabulary or RIC, during her visit to the Castle in 1861, in appreciation of their role in subduing the Fenian rebellion earlier that year (see image on p.91) which, as with the previous rising of 1848, had been foiled because of informers.

Drummond also reformed the Dublin Night Watch by creating the Dublin Metropolitan Police (DMP), which he modelled on Peel's London Metropolitan Police. This was an unarmed force with an armed detective G Division (at 5 Exchange Court, immediately behind the Treasury building) which investigated serious lawbreaking, including political crime.

above Old Police Office (with Police Barracks Yard through archway, Armoury and Back Avenue to right) by Pat Liddy.

(He is remembered as a reforming administrator and his statue is located prominently in City Hall, with his motto: 'Property has its duties as well as its rights' carved on the pedestal.)

On 5th January 1838, 800 men of the DMP paraded in frock coats and top hats reinforced with whalebone, which by standing on them, enabled officers to see over obstructions. [66] They were inspected by Lord Lieutenant Constantine Phipps (1835-39) to whom Dublin was described in the new Commissioner's first report as 'a lawless city, criminals having usurped control over a considerable portion of their fellow citizens' and was advised that certain specified areas were 'hotbeds of human turpitude'. The *Dublin Evening Post* declared the parade to have 'altogether presented a very uniform as well as a very efficient appearance'. The Castle Police Office (1838, as shown) was their Dublin Metropolitan Area Headquarters, where the 'orders of the day' were copied and delivered to all seven Dublin districts. The transcribers had to 'write them into the books at the station houses' and were responsible for ensuring 'that there is no bad spelling and that the orders are copied correctly'

Following the handover of political power to the new Provisional Irish Government, the newly formed unarmed Civic Guard marched through Palace Street Gate to take possession on 17th August 1922. The Garda Síochána have retained their presence in the Police Barracks Yard ever since.

The Dublin Street Directory of 1850 gives extensive information on the occupancy of the Castle. The **Upper Castle Yard** housed the Privy Council Chamber and offices and rooms of the Chief Secretary, Law Officers, Loan Fund Board, Lunatic Inspectors, Officers of the Household and Master of the Ceremonies. There was also a maze of servants' stores and quarters 'behind the scenes' – including lamp and brushing rooms, glass, plate and pastry pantries, larders, sculleries, kitchens and wine cellars.

The **Lower Castle Yard** (comprising everywhere not in the Upper Castle Yard) accommodated the Aide-de-Camps' quarters, Castle Mews, and offices of the Paymaster of the Civil Service, Loan Fund Board, Prison Inspector, Quartermaster-General, Ordnance Department, Metropolitan Police Commissioner and the Office of Arms. The cavalry were housed in the Piquet Yard at Palace Gate – diagonally opposite the riding school, stables and forge.

This Directory also shows the economic and social effects of the Castle on its surroundings: **Dame Street** had many fashionable shops which catered for Castle courtiers and the wealthy. Premises included a button maker 'to the

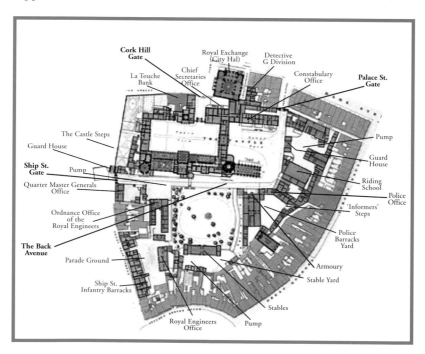

above The Castle from Ordnance Survey Map, 1843, annotated.

Lord Lieutenant', wine, spirits, tobacco and snuff merchants, gun manufacturers and that of Mr John Michaels – 'Furrier to Viceroy and Vicereine Clarendon'.

Castle Street housed confectioners, tailors, drapers, lace makers, glovers, bonnet and hat shops, chemists and druggists, solicitors' and barristers' offices, taverns and the La Touche and Newcomen Banks.

Ship Street (at the back of the Castle) had grocers, provisions dealers, dairies, a coal yard, a timber merchant, shoe, boot and watch-case makers, a printer, engravers, wire works, a French 'stay and corset maker' and a fireproof safe manufacturer. (A number of houses were demolished in Little Ship at this time, to make way for road widening.)

The close working proximity and pattern of office arrangements of the Castle's 'law and order top brass' was described graphically by a commentator in 1912: 'The Chief Secretary's room opens into the Under-Secretary's and the Under-Secretary's into the Assistant Under-Secretary's. In the passage outside to the right is the Council Chamber, where the Privy Council assembles as occasion demands. At the other end of the passage are the Law Officers' departments. The Attorney General and Solicitor General sit in one room and this opens into the Lord Chancellor's Room. A short stone staircase outside the Lord Chancellor's room leads to the apartments (opening into each other) of the Inspector-General and Deputy Inspector-General of the Constabulary… In the Lower Castle Yard are the offices of the Chief Commissioner and Assistant Commissioner of the Metropolitan Police.' [67]

The Castle during 'The Great Hunger'

The Irish Potato Famine of 1845-1849, also known as 'the Great Hunger', was the greatest social tragedy in Irish history and the only major famine in modern European history. The widespread adoption of the potato had been made out of necessity during periods of systematic destruction of corn crops by Crown forces two centuries previously. Since the mid 1700s, the population had doubled to nine million – one third of which were Irish speaking labourers, small cottiers or subsistence farmers. (The Irish language was already under threat by its compulsory exclusion from national schools and the progress of English – the language of commerce and social advancement.) They were totally dependent on this staple, high-yielding, but unreliable wonder crop to feed themselves, their families, fowls and pigs.

The potato blight (*phytophthora infestans*) affected most of Western Europe in 1845, but repeated crop failures in Ireland delivered a mortal blow to those at the lowest levels of the economic pyramid, as none owned their own land and their grain 'cash crops' went to pay the rent. It was a disease unknown to scientists and only a minority of horticulturalists correctly identified its cause as a parasitical fungus. Viceroy Heytesbury (1844-46) established a three-man commission – none of whom had practical agricultural experience – which reported that it was brought about by excessively wet summer weather and that the mould merely accompanied the disease. [68] This, and other such erroneous findings, delayed scientific research and a preventative copper sulphate solution wasn't introduced for a further forty years.

Dublin escaped the worst horrors of starvation, but large numbers of refugees, fleeing rural areas, emigrated through its port and the Castle authorities feared that a huge influx of vagrants would flood the town. Some bakeries were looted and there were a number of food riots. In one incident, of eight men arrested from a mob of 300, only one was from the locality. More than 2,000 paupers, 'wallowing in mud', received food, lodgings and work at the poorhouse in James's Street, 2km west of the Castle. Sir Charles Trevelyan, the Permanent Secretary at the British Treasury with responsibility for the social and economic policy in Ireland, expressed his hope 'since provision is made for the poor, the inhabitants of Dublin will discourage all vagrant beggars and give their assistance that they may be sent to bridewell to hard labour and thereby free themselves from a set of idlers who are a scandal and a reproach to the nation.'

Dublin's population increased (reaching 260,000 by 1852) despite the dramatic plunge in the national population and the town's high death rate and very high infant mortality rate. Competition for housing was intense among the poor. The capital also suffered serious outbreaks of the diseases that accompanied the famine – including typhus, dysentery and yellow fever. Highly infectious smallpox was also rampant.

Trevelyan may have been conscientious but was not very humane in his rigid application of laissez faire, insisting that market

below 'Trouping of the Colours', St. Patrick's Day 1844, with the 11th Hussars to right, 10th Infantry to left foreground, and Chief Secretary's Offices at back right, by Michael Angelo Hayes.

forces, should prevail and must never be interfered with – neither in commercial (including food exports) nor social contexts. This policy was responsible for many deaths. In common with most of his Whig (Liberal) Party colleagues, he adhered obsessively to the evangelical providentialist doctrine that God directed human affairs for the ultimate good of humanity: 'The cure has been applied by the direct stroke of an all wise Providence'. [69] Many starving Irish later came to share this belief.

The Irish Executive increasingly held contrary views to Trevelyan and the United Kingdom Government, and demanded State intervention with humanitarian aid. George Villiers, Earl of Clarendon, who had viewed the nationwide crisis as the result of the moral failings of the Irish, completely changed his opinions shortly after his appointment as Lord Lieutenant (1847-52). He came under the influence of the senior administrators in the Castle and acknowledged that the preservation of human life was imperative, both on compassionate and political grounds. [70]

Viceroy Clarendon invited Alexis Soyer, the French chef of London's Reform Club, for a gala launch of a new soup-kitchen scheme. Soyer's assertion that bread and a nourishing bowl of beef, flour, barley and dripping soup would sustain a man for a day, was put into effect at Croppies' Acre, Wolfe Tone Quay. The scheme was a success and some three million people were in receipt of daily rations countrywide that August. But, it was discontinued after its first year of operation as the U.K. Government mistakenly adjudged the famine to have ended.

Clarendon then convinced Prime Minister John Russell to come to Dublin that September (1848) to finalise his plans to counter the escalating human tragedy. But these and all Lord Russell's other plans failed. [71]

Many traders had been ruined and the Viceroy encouraged the visit of Queen Victoria, in the hope that it would build confidence and stimulate commerce. However, an Asiatic cholera epidemic erupted, spread quickly in the congested city, decimated the Ship Street Ordnance garrison and placed the journey in jeopardy. On August 6th 1849, Queen Victoria arrived at Kingstown (now Dún Laoghaire) Co. Dublin, accompanied by their Royal Highnesses the Prince Consort, the Prince of Wales and the Princess Royal. She did not acknowledge the famine in her correspondence, but, in a letter to her Uncle Leopold, King of the Belgians, she wrote: 'you see more ragged and wretched people here

above *State Ball in St. Patrick's Hall, c.1850, with Lord and Lady Clarendon on dais and officers with partners in foreground.*

than I ever saw anywhere else... Tomorrow we have a Levée [in the Castle] where 1,700 are to be presented and the next day a review [of the troops] and in the evening the Drawing Room, where 900 ladies are to be presented.' The visit passed off without the slightest incident – in contrast to her third one in 1861, during which there were street protests and stones were thrown at Prince Albert.

It is estimated that 1.5 million people died and 1.5 million emigrated during the course of the famine. North America and Australia were the most favoured destinations for both sexes of all classes and this pattern continued far into the twentieth century.

Ireland had not been governed as a full member of the U.K., but had been abandoned by a government that continually did too little too late and that doomed the unhappy union of Great Britain and Ireland.

On 1st June 1997, Tony Blair, Prime Minister of the United Kingdom, expressed deep regret for the Great Famine "that still causes pain as we reflect on it today. Those who governed in London at the time failed their people through standing by while a crop failure turned into a massive human tragedy. It is also right that we should pay tribute to the ways in which the Irish people have triumphed in the face of this catastrophe."

The Castle Social Scene and the Ebbing Tide

above Going to the Levée, by Rose Barton.

aspiring gentry, debutantes and mothers from the great houses of Ireland eagerly awaited the Viceroy's gilt-edged, hand-delivered invitation to attend.

The Viceroy's levée opened the proceedings with 'a parading of the men of court'. On that evening, 'Dame Street was packed from end to end' with a stream of carriages and 'outside cars' leading to Cork Hill Gate. 'They are of all sorts and condition, from the hansome brougham which conveys the Lord Chancellor in his wig and gown, to the jarvey upon which lounge a couple of officers in resplendent uniform.' [72]

Carriage parking was always strictly regulated and could entail long delays both on arrival and departure. Some guests travelled in 'inside cars' and, on one such occasion, the policeman on duty

The most important period in Dublin's social calendar was the six festive weeks of the Castle's balls and dinners, which culminated in the Grand Ball on St Patrick's night, 17th March. During this 'Castle Season', the Viceroy resided in the Castle with his own furniture, gold plate and retinue. Dublin hotel and boarding rooms were booked far in advance. Gentry,

LEVEE

5th FEBRUARY, 1889.

Pass the Carriage of

The Right Hon. the Lord Mayor

through Ship St. Gate to the Private Entrée Door.

The Police on Duty.

The Chief Commissioner of Police.

above Lord Mayor's coach pass for 5th February 1889, which allowed access via Ship Street Gate to private entrée door.

directing the carriages repeatedly shouted: 'Mrs A, B, or C's inside is coming up.' [73] This was greeted with much merriment by the onlookers.

That levée 'is but an inferior occasion when compared with the Ladies Drawing Room of the second [Wednesday] evening when the Castle is a scene of wonderful animation. The windows blaze with light, scarlet cloth covers the staircase and corridors, which are filled with lovely debutantes and handsome matrons. There is a frou frou of silken dresses and the chatter of many voices. There is the crowding into the antechamber, the passing into the pen. [74] Elizabeth Burke, a 16 year old debutante from Co. Galway, recalled being presented to Viceroy Spencer, who was in court dress with 'glittering orders', in the 'picturesque' Throne Room during the 1882 season: 'It is the beard that I remember. In those days the Lord Lieutenant kissed each of the debutantes as they were presented – an ordeal for both. I can remember now the feeling of that long thick red beard against my cheek, tickling it. Then it is over and now I curtsy to the lovely golden haired, rose and white, but rather pompous-looking lady in her glittering jewels, beside Lord Spencer, and walk backwards a few steps as I have been taught to do; without, I pray, falling over my train. An A.D.C. picks it up and

replaces it on my arm, and the ceremony is over. In the long [Picture] gallery, refreshments are served, and one meets one's friends as at an ordinary evening party.' [75]

She was also aware of her position in relation to society at large: 'There was a crowd about the gates of the Castle. The Dublin poor always turned out to see any sight that there was. They shivered on the pavement in their thin, ragged clothes, waiting for hours sometimes, so that they might see the ladies in their silks and satins and furs step from their carriages into the warmth and light and gaiety that received them. The poor were incredibly patient. Even then

above *Lord Lieutenant John Poyntz Spencer (1868-74 and 82-85 with his thick 'tickly' beard.*

I was dimly aware of the appalling contrast between their lives and ours, and wondered how long they would remain patient.' The reminiscences of an another eyewitness, however, suggests that the crowd could be less than patient: 'The motley throng in the sidewalks indulges their pungent wit, not unmixed with sarcasm, at the expense of each individual as he goes by.' [76]

(Elizabeth got engaged in her 'very first season' and in May of the following year, became Countess Fingall and wife of the 24 year old 11th Earl – who had inherited a seat in the House of Lords and was heir to three peerages.)

Banquets were hosted on the following evenings, followed by small, intimate dances in the Throne Room – 'invitations to which are eagerly coveted'. The grand State Ball was held on Saturday night and then this pattern of functions repeated.

Madam, the pen name of another invitee, described the table arrangements in St. Patrick's Hall during the 1892 Season. In the centre of the room, overshadowed by two spreading palms, was a round 'top table' reserved for the Viceregal party. Radiating from there, four long 'arms' of tables, with 'islands of same all down them, varied by full many a magnificent racing cup and centre piece –

trophies from [Lord Lieutenant, 1889-92] Lord Zetland's success on the turf'.

At 9.30 pm, following dinner and the playing of the National Anthem [*God save the Queen*], the guests 'filed back to the Drawing room, where the other guests invited for the dance were beginning to arrive'. This interlude presented a further opportunity for socialising at what was unkindly described as the Castle marriage market – 'each man on arriving, having been given a card with his partner's name and being introduced if necessary'. The Viceregal party also withdrew – the ladies to the Reserved Supper (Bermingham Tower) Room for tea, sherry and conversation, while their male companions smoked cigars, drank port and brandy and played billiards in the adjoining Wedgewood Room.

When Madam returned to St. Patrick's Hall soon after midnight, she found the 'beautiful elaborate table gone like last year's snow and in its place a large centre table for their excellencies, etc. and several smaller ones all beautifully arranged with flowers and an elaborate supper, while the tall palms – no joke to move – form groups at the end of the room'. On enquiring of a member of staff, she was informed that more than 15,000 guests were entertained

above *Military march past in 'slow time'.*

during the Castle Season 'and
judging from what I have seen on
many occasions there, well
entertained too'. [77]

It was customary for the Viceroy
to 'make merry and drown the
shamrock' on St. Patrick's Day. It
began with inspection of the guard
and military manoeuvres, by the
Viceroy and his festively dressed
entourage on the (since removed)
Throne Room balcony. That night,
a gala banquet was held, followed
by the grand finale – St Patrick's

Ball, 'in the hall of that name which
hardly holds the crowd of dancers.'

As might be expected, when the
Viceroy and Vicereine were generous
in their patronage and largess, they
were generally popular in
fashionable society and greatly in
demand at public gatherings such
as flower shows, bazaars and the
theatre. He felt obliged not only to
spend the full amount of his highly
paid annual salary on official
entertainment, but his social
standing was judged on what was
spent in addition to this. Lord
Lieutenant Aberdeen (1886 and

1905-14) estimated that he annually spent £7,000 of his own money on hospitality, over and above his £20,000 salary, during his second term of office (see his photo on p.81).

He and Lady Aberdeen displayed a new, more egalitarian approach and were popular with the 'ordinary people'. *The Irish Times* (which had strong Unionist leanings and later turned against them) wrote that 'they entertained the kindest feelings towards all classes in the country'.

The couple hosted a ball in the Castle for the servants of the Viceregal Court and their friends on Wednesday, 10th March 1886, which the *Court Society Review* reported disapprovingly: It 'was probably the first instance of a Lady Lieutenant descending from the pedestal of her dignity to inaugurate the amusements of her dependants.'

Viceroy Aberdeen enthusiastically supported 'Home Rule' (a domestic Parliament for home affairs, under

above *Vicereine Ishbel Aberdeen, 1886.*

the British Crown) and consequently, was unpopular with Unionists, including the majority of the Castle administration, and was subjected to constant criticism by both ends of the political spectrum. To the great annoyance of King Edward VII, many of the ascendancy refused to attend the Viceregal Court 'on principle' during his second term. Their places were taken by army officers and professionals. Nevertheless, it was described in 1907 as 'though shorn of some of its eighteenth-century magnificence, is wanting neither in dignity nor in social attractiveness'. In reality, however, the days of the Castle Court (and of British rule) were coming to an end.

Ishbel Aberdeen was the most remarkable of the Vicereines. She disliked 'the stifling official artificiality that required her to wear a perpetual smile', and the continual round of social engagements and official entertaining that were an integral part of her symbolic and ceremonial role as representative of the pageantry of the monarchy and manipulator of public opinion. She also hated the restrictions of being unable to walk outside the Castle grounds and of constantly being accompanied by armed detectives.[78] (Such strict security was deemed necessary in view of the shocking assassination of Under Secretary Thomas Henry Burke and newly

arrived Chief Secretary Frederick Cavendish, in the Phoenix Park on 6th May 1882.)

There was a tradition of Vicereines promoting charities of their choice. Lady Londonderry (1886-89) had sponsored tweed and lace making and Lady Dudley (1902-1905) had supported a scheme of nursing for the poor. Ishbel was determined to put her vigorous personality and Christian beliefs to good effect and continued the promotion of local industry, became president of the Irish Home Industries Association and developed outlets and market-led products – as even a small extra income to a family could 'keep the wolf from the door'. Her 'crusade', was the elimination of the 'white plague' of tuberculosis, which she knew to be exacerbated by inadequate, insanitary housing conditions (and on which she robustly challenged the government). She tackled this with practical works – including the establishment of Peamount Hospital, Co. Dublin, to which she remained a life-long patron.

She was President of the International Council of Women for over forty years, but during her terms of public office limited her announcements on women's suffrage to statements such as 'women should [be allowed to] do their duty' and that 'she longed for the day when the law will recognise

106

no sex'. Queen Victoria didn't favour women voting, but had tolerated this contrary conviction in her Vicereine. Later in life, Ishbel demanded equal voting rights. [79]

We can imagine her ambivalence in relation to the incident that took place at Ship Street Barracks at 5.30 am on 13th April 1912, when four suffragettes broke nineteen windows 'as a protest against the Government' and were arrested. Constable 119B gave evidence that he had witnessed the two Miss Murphys throwing stones and Mrs Hannah Sheehy-Skeffington and Mrs Margaret Palmer 'using sticks on the windows – the property of the War Department'. Damage was

estimated at thirty shillings. Chief Magistrate Swift convicted them of 'glass breaking in public buildings' and sentenced each to forty shillings' fine or one month in prison. All chose prison.

Although Sheehy-Skeffington's medical adviser reported that her deteriorating health had become such as to render immediate release advisable, she was detained a further night – despite the concern of the Aberdeens for her plight. According to *The Irish Citizen* ('For Men and Women Equally the Rights and Duties of Citizenship'), this act of petty malice against feminist militants in the cause of the universal franchise 'originated with the permanent officials in Dublin Castle – either Mr Max Green, Chairman of the Prisons Board or Sir James Dougherty, Undersecretary'. [80] (Hannah's husband, Francis Sheehy-Skeffington – a well known pacifist, was arrested while trying to prevent looting during the Easter Rising, held hostage and summarily executed in Portobello Barracks.)

The last State ceremonial departure of a Viceroy took place from the Castle on 15th February 1915. The newly invested Marquis of Aberdeen and Temair (the Irish name for Tara the seat of the ancient High Kings – meaning 'dark earth goddess') rode at the forefront of the procession in formal dress. Further back, heartbroken Ishbel, who had grown to love Ireland, took photographs of the cheering crowds from the State carriage. 'Ireland had been the centre of our lives', she wrote. So, perhaps it was appropriate that their departure wasn't delayed, as the nationalist political scene had evolved, intensified and escalated dramatically in the almost thirty years since their first term, and the future could hold no such official role for them. A distinct generation gap had emerged and the young were more radical, held militant separatist ambitions, and had confidence in their ability to achieve it. Home Rule – the objective of nationalists for almost fifty years – was now no longer enough.

Royal visits had increased dramatically in reaction to these political developments and were carefully stage-managed to win public support for the Viceregal Court, the Irish Executive and the Union. In 1895, the Prince of Wales officiated at a levée and ladies drawing room at the Castle. In August 1897, Prince George, Duke of York, accompanied by the Duchess, took the oath of membership of the Privy Council in their chamber and was invested as a Knight of St. Patrick at a magnificent ceremony in St. Patrick's Hall 'that was as impressive as ever.'[81] Queen Victoria paid her fourth and final visit in April 1900 – the year before her death. Three years later, the visit of King Edward VII was opposed by the National Council, but he again made state visits with Queen Alexandra in 1904 and 1907. The last Royal visitors were Queen Mary and George V, King of the United Kingdom of Great Britain, Ireland and Emperor of India in 1911. They officiated at a levée, the investiture of some Knights of St. Patrick and a State banquet, and 'basked in Dublin's warm welcome'.

The novelist and short-story writer, Séan O'Faoláin, (1900-99, who was the son of an RIC Constable and became a member of the IRA during the 'Troubles') remembered how he too 'gloried in all the trappings, Kings, Queens, Dukes, Duchesses, Generals, Admirals, Soldiers, Sailors, Colonists and Conquerors – the lot!'

The 'Troubles' and End of British Rule

above: The State Drawing Room. *left:* *in nineteenth century.* *centre:* *in use as military hospital in 1916.* *right:* *today.*

Britain entered the First World War in August 1914, on the side of the Franco-Russian alliance and in opposition to Germany and the Austro-Hungarian Empire. Prime Minister Asquith explained this, not in terms of British strategic and imperial interests, but that 'Britain was fighting to uphold international law and the rights of small nations.' [82] The moderate Irish Parliamentary Party pledged the support of its followers to the war effort (as did the Ulster Unionists) in the expectation that loyalty would be compensated and Home Rule would be granted afterwards. Almost 300,000 Irishmen 'answered the call' and 50,000 died in the British army during this 'war to end wars'.

Most 'physical-force nationalists', however, believed that self-government would never be willingly granted and began to make serious preparations for another rebellion – that of Easter 1916. Training was done in the hills and night-time street fighting manoeuvres became a regular occurrence in Dublin at weekends – including occasional mimic attacks on the Castle – with little police intervention. Military exercises by over 2,000 Irish National Volunteers (a radical militia) brought city-centre traffic to a standstill on the 17th March 1916. Many of them were armed and a manifesto had been issued warning that 'attempted disarming...can only be met by resistance and bloodshed'.

Sir Matthew Nathan, Under Secretary and member of the Irish Privy Council, wrote to the Prime Minister from the Castle on 10th April, assuring him that: 'although the Irish Volunteers element has been active of late, especially in Dublin, I do not believe that its leaders mean insurrection or that the volunteers have sufficient arms if the leaders do mean it.' Major Ivor H. Price, Intelligence Officer attached to the Irish Command disagreed and maintained that Sinn Féin Volunteers (the radical nationalist party) were 'working up for rebellion'. Lord Lieutenant Wimborne (1915-18) was of the same opinion as Price – especially in view of a recent seizure of a quantity of grenades and bayonets. However, Chief Secretary Augustine Birrell, who had held office for nine years, thought that the idea was rubbish: "I laugh at the whole thing" He was confident that deportation of the leaders of the movement would defuse the situation should it deteriorate further and instructed Colonel Edgeworth-Johnstone, Chief Commissioner of the DMP, to 'keep turbulent suspects under close observation.'

The Volunteers had planned a general mobilisation for Easter Sunday 23rd April, but their moderate Commander in Chief, Eoin MacNeill, learnt that the radical Irish Republican Brotherhood element in the leadership was about to exploit it to activate widespread insurrection and posted notices of cancellation in the Saturday national newspapers. An informer in the Volunteers assured Nathan that, there was now no possibility of an Easter rising.

No mass gathering occurred, but that morning an armed robbery of 250 lbs.(113 kg) of gelignite took place at a quarry in Co. Dublin and it was reported that all or part of the haul had been taken to Liberty Hall, the headquarters of the Citizen Army (a Socialist Militia pledged to work for an Irish Republic and the emancipation of labour) which was known to be acting in combination with the Volunteers. An emergency meeting was held at the Castle where it was decided to arrest the leaders on grounds of 'hostile association' and to raid Liberty Hall the following Tuesday – as there would be too many holidaymakers in town the next day, a public holiday and Nathan felt that the Government's (that is the Chief Secretary's) authorisation was required. [83]

That Sunday evening, the Citizen Army was led on a final route march past the Castle by their commandant, James Connolly, while bomb making continued unabated in Liberty Hall. Nathan wired Birrell (who was in London at a cabinet crisis) advising him that he was now in agreement with Viceroy Wimborne and proposed that all the leaders be immediately interned in England: 'Can this be proceeded with, subject to concurrence of law officers, military authorities and Home Office?' He also complained of lack of co-operation from the Intelligence Service and that he wasn't getting enough information 'about what was going on'. (Indeed, much of their intelligence was incorrect.) Early next day, 24th April, the Chief Secretary approved this proposed course of action. It was too late.

The (much smaller than planned) Easter Rising began that morning and was largely confined to Dublin. Only the determined rebel 'hard core' participated, in the firm belief that their generation would be disgraced forever if they failed to seize the moment to strike for independence – 'England's difficulty being Ireland's opportunity'. Strategic buildings were simultaneously seized at gunpoint and holes were bored in adjoining walls. The General Post Office (O'Connell Street) became their central fortress from where they proclaimed the Irish Republic as a sovereign independent state.

One of the first fatalities was Constable James O'Brien, who was shot through the head at 12.10 pm as he tried to shut the Castle's Cork Hill Gate on twenty-five advancing Citizen Army fighters (which included nine women). Their advantage was not used effectively, as hesitating, they lost the element of surprise and a sentry slammed the gate shut. A grenade was lobbed at the Guard House door, shattered a pain of glass, but failed to explode. (The Guard House now forms part of Dublin Castle Conference Centre's dining facilities and the bayonet marks made by the British sentries can still be plainly seen.)

below Cork Hill Gate – with sentry and police man. Guard House is to left, City Hall to right and Dame Street in distance.

They withdrew to City Hall, where their snipers overlooked the Chief Secretary's and Prison Board Offices and large sections of the Upper Castle Yard, and to the *Daily Express* and *Evening Mail* building, on the corner of Dame Street and Parliament Street, which also provided direct line of fire on Cork Hill Gate – as it appeared foolhardy to attempt an attack on the 'wide open spaces' of the Upper Castle Yard, especially in view of the anticipated large number of troops stationed in Ship Street Barracks.

However, the attack had been a total surprise to the authorities and the Castle was inadequately defended by only seventy raw recruits. The regular complement was a company of 200 soldiers – some of whom were a billeted detachment of Royal Inniskillings Fusiliers on the way to the Western Front. (They were later rotated with a company from the Shropshire Regiment, who were present at the final hand over to Irish Free State forces.) In addition, there were routinely twenty-four armed RIC sentries and bodyguards to the Viceroy. According to the press, the majority were at the Fairyhouse races, believing the rebellion to have been aborted. Nathan, accompanied by the storekeeper, had to break into the armoury but only obtained revolvers, for which he could not find ammunition, to

James Connolly, by Séan O'Sullivan – State Apartments. His motto was 'We serve neither King nor Kaiser - but Ireland'

arm the Castle Constables.

The first rebel fatality was Captain Séan Connolly, a professional actor, who had shot Constable O'Brien. He was hit by sniper fire from troops on the roof of Bedford Tower, while raising the tricolour over City Hall. James Connolly had wished him 'good luck' at the general, combined, mobilisation at Liberty Hall and parted with the words: "we won't meet again".

All available troops from Royal, Richmond and Portabello Barracks were rushed to reinforce the Castle garrison. A battalion of South Staffords from the Curragh Camp arrived during the afternoon. They had been delayed by street barricades and lost several men through sniper fire on their march from Kingsbridge (now Heuston) Station and were to lose two more in the Upper Castle Yard in the same manner, during the course of the week. At 5 pm, they raked City Hall with machine gunfire and then captured it in a charge by troops with fixed bayonets. The following night, following the arrival of a battery of '18 pounder' guns from Athlone, the *Daily Express* and *Evening Mail* and 'adjacent occupied buildings' adjacent were subjected to a heavy bombardment from the Castle and were successfully stormed by a detachment of the 5th Royal Dublin Fuliers. *The Irish Times* reported that twenty-four bodies were recovered.

Vicereine Aberdeen's plan to equip the State Apartments as a Red Cross Hospital for war wounded soldiers and sailors had been put into effect and seventy patients from the front lines (quarter full capacity) were lodged there on Easter Monday. Many nurses were off duty and unable to return, but one from the Voluntary Aid Detachment (an auxiliary organisation) wrote a dramatic eyewitness account of the Castle during that week of heavy fighting. All the beds were moved from the Picture Gallery and the Throne Room to St. Patrick's Hall and the corridors and landings 'at the back of the house'. Blinds were closed, lights turned off and all operations cancelled during the first two, most hazardous days. (The gas supply remained off for the week). There was a constant stream of ambulances, covered carts, stretchers and armoured motorcars going in and out of the yard. The dead had their faces covered. All day long twenty soldiers dug graves in the Castle Garden – officers were buried separately, and there were two large graves for "Tommies" and "Sinn Féiners". Funerals took place each evening after dark and most were buried in sheets.' (All were later re-interred elsewhere).

Troops not on duty sat around a

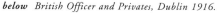

below British Officer and Privates, Dublin 1916.

fire in the Battleaxe Landing (see photo p.133) while others slept in ornamental palms and plant 'baths' (three at either end), in the matron's office where a billygoat – the regimental mascot of the Light Infantry, and the 4th Hussars' bulldog had come uninvited, in the boiler room or wherever they could.[84] In all, one hundred and eighty wounded soldiers, twenty-four rebels and twenty civilians were brought to the hospital in the State Apartments and thirty-six died.

John Samuel Carrothers, a 2nd Lieutenant with the 3rd Battalion of the Inniskillings, was stationed in Ship Street Barracks that week. (He was to die in action at Passchendaele [Third Battle of Ypres] Belgium on 16th August 1917) The following are extracts from the remarkable letters he wrote to his mother in Farnaght, Tamlaght, Co. Fermanagh.[85]

Wednesday 26th April: a 'good many prisoners were brought in here–some badly wounded. We have nearly a dozen women prisoners in this barracks alone [some of whom had been captured in City Hall]. The Sinn Féiners are constantly sniping from the roofs... More reinforcements have arrived from England... I am fed up being confined to barracks. We are overcrowded and always sleep in our clothes, with rifle and bayonet beside us... We are cut off from the outside world entirely'.

Thursday 27th: 'I was on a grave digging party, but as soon as we started work we were sniped at. Some chaps got into the graves but I saw that we were been taken at a disadvantage and you would not have seen me for the dust I kicked up running away. Two snipers appeared at a chimney quite close and we opened fire on them. The chimney fell and also both the snipers. One was only wounded and he was brought in as a prisoner. His coat was covered in blood and brains of the other sniper. A sight like this puts the notion of war out of ones head'.

Saturday 29th: 'There is a great cheering now, we have just been told that the Sinn Féiners have tendered an unconditional surrender... Snipers are still firing... I had my clothes off for the first time last night and also got a decent sleep for the first time. I also had a shave to-day, but I had to use a basin of clear water as a looking glass, so you may guess we are living under war conditions. I have seen enough of the horrors of war without going to France to see any more'.

Sunday 30th: 'Prisoners are being brought in in hundreds... The Russian Countess who led this rebellion [Constance Markievicz, nee Gore-Booth, – a Citizen Army commander in the St. Stephen's Green area] was brought in here as a prisoner today... These barracks are part of Dublin Castle and it is the headquarters of the whole campaign. I was through the Castle today. It shows the traces of fighting. The great marble staircases are torn with bullets and pools of clotted blood are at almost every door. The hospital is full of wounded. Important papers are being trampled over and office accoutrements are scattered everywhere... There is a heavy smell about the city – the smell of blood and of corpses... The weather is and has been very hot and sultry...No Irish men need look for a job in England now as we are considered worse than the Germans by the troops over from England and Wales'.

That same afternoon, the V.A.D. nurse 'could not help but notice the flurry of interest when James Connolly was stretchered in, with three of his men on either side and guarded by thirty British soldiers.' After a ten minute discussion, he was brought to a room in the officers quarters of the State Apartments (that had previously been reserved for royalty and is now the James Connolly Room) and there detained with 'an armed sentry outside each door and another in the room'. His leg was dressed and re-splinted – the tibia and fibula having been shattered by sniper fire three days previously. He was given a copy of Pádraig Pearses' order of surrender to the Volunteers and issued a similar one to his combatants.

Family visits were forbidden at first. According to his daughter, Nora, 'she tried and tried, but it was no use. I stopped a nurse I saw coming out [of Cork Hill] and asked her if she could give me any news. She said daddy was very weak; he had lost a lot of blood'.

below British army sentry and soldiers in parade ground at Ship Street Barracks (looking north to Ship Street Gate. See Ship Street frontage p.88).

Gangrene had set in. The Castle doctors were consulted and certified that he was 'perfectly rational and in full possession of his faculties…his mind, memory and understanding entirely unimpaired' and fit to undergo trial.

On Tuesday morning, 9th May, prisoner number 90 was courtmartialled by three military judges, while 'propped up in his bed'. Connolly entered a plea of not guilty to the charges that he: 'Did an act to wit did take part in an armed rebellion and in the waging of war against His Majesty the King, such act being of such a nature as to be calculated to be prejudicial to the Defence of the Realm and being done with the intention and for the purpose of assisting the enemy'. Secondly, that he: 'Did attempt to cause disaffection among the civilian population of His Majesty'.

The prosecution called four military witnesses who gave evidence that he had exercised military command. He cross-examined two of them (one of whom had been tied up in a telephone box for three hours, on his instructions) and was dismissive of their 'trifling allegations' of cruelty – insisting that such incidents were unavoidable in the circumstances. Reading from a prepared script, he asserted that "British control of Ireland was usurpation" and that "we succeeded in proving that Irishmen are ready to die endeavouring to win for Ireland their national rights which the British government has been asking them to die to win for Belgium". Major Woodward, Lieutenant Colonel Bent and Colonel Sapte found him guilty on the first charge and surprisingly, not guilty on the second.

His wife Lillie was allowed a short visit that evening – having promised not to tell him of the series of executions of the other leaders and following a search for anything 'with which he could take his own life'. She found that James could only move his head and shoulders and a cage held up the bedclothes above his leg. He told her that the strain of the courts martial had been very great, but was overjoyed to hear that their fifteen year son, Roddy, had been released after eight days detention in Richmond Barracks.

Major General Maxwell, Commander in Chief of the Home Command, who had been appointed on 27th April with complete authority to crush the rebellion, confirmed the imposition of the 'extreme penalty' and the execution was fixed for dawn on the 11th. It was suspended for 24 hours by the Prime Minister, who, during a Parliamentary debate in the House of Commons that same day, announced the continuance of the executions and said that as Connolly had taken "the most active part of all in the actual rebellion in Dublin...I do not see my way to interfere with the decision of Sir John Maxwell". John Dillon, the succeeding leader of the – now doomed – Irish Parliamentary Party, declared his bitter opposition to this policy: "It is the first rebellion that ever took place in Ireland where you had the majority on your side...Now you are washing out our whole life work in a sea of blood". Laurence Ginnell, his more radical party colleague, shouted that these executions were simply "murders" and demanded to know by what precedent Herbert Henry Asquith intended killing a dying man.

Lillie received an urgent message around midnight, that requested her to attend the Castle immediately. She and Nora were driven by ambulance through curfew enforced darkened and deserted streets, where there was 'not a sole to be seen, not even a soldier'. James was to be executed 'in the early hours' and had received confession. He was shocked at the news of the executions of his colleagues – having believed that he was to be the first, and fell silent for a while. Then he replied: "hasn't it been a full life, Lillie, and isn't this a good end?" She collapsed when the soldier announced: "you've only five minutes more". According to the V.A.D. nurse, throughout his detention James's behaviour was that of an idealist and he was calm and composed throughout – until it came to say goodbye. At 3.30 am he was carried down the imperial staircase to a waiting ambulance and driven to Kilmainham Gaol, where he was strapped to a chair and executed by firing squad. (One medical eyewitness claimed that he had suffered a heart attack and died in the ambulance.)

Though the rebellion was initially unpopular with the general population (many prisoners had abuse and objects flung at them as they were led into captivity) the series of fifteen executions spread over ten days – which culminated with the death of Connolly – caused public anger to change to sympathy for their cause. The authorities had hoped that they would act as a deterrent to others, but this policy backfired and rapidly enflamed resentment among the majority. It awoke a dormant spirit of nationalism and caused a major shift in public support away from the moderate Home Rulers to the radical separatist movement – so ensuring that the Easter Rising became only 'round one' – the seminal event in the struggle for Irish independence.

Chief Secretary Birrell had sailed back to Dublin on a battleship on

Easter Monday and 'drove through a fusillade of shots' to his residence in the Phoenix Park, where he remained until he resigned the following Sunday. Under Secretary Nathan 'followed suit' three days later and was reassigned to supervision of defensive trench works in the South of England. Soon afterwards, he wrote that he favoured the creation of a movement in Ireland for the maintenance of the British connection and also the development of the national individuality of Ireland: 'It has been one of the Government's mistakes to treat the latter purpose as essentially antagonistic to the former, with the result that they have made it so.' His Civil Service career was later to progress again. Viceroy Wimbourne initially resisted but eventually resigned on the 7th May, as the British Cabinet demanded a complete change of personnel in the Irish Executive.

The Royal Commission appointed to investigate the facts surrounding the rebellion opened at the Royal Commissioners' House, Westminster on 18th May, under the chairmanship of Lord Hardinge and heard nine days of testimony. Birrell was questioned at length and didn't perform well. He explained that he held the view that he should attend all cabinet meetings "in order to see whether Ireland was affected. Bills are sometimes instituted in a great hurry and Ireland is either left out or put in without any consideration whatsoever of her needs or history". He admitted intelligence failures, especially among the Castle's G Division and explained that they didn't disarm the Volunteers as the Cabinet hadn't moved against the

below Matthew Nathan, ex Under Secretary for Ireland and Augustine Birrell, ex Chief Secretary, leaving the Royal Commission hearings.

Ulster Volunteer Force (who had armed to prevent Home Rule in April 1914) and that to do so would have "completely alienated nationalist opinion and with it that large body of Irish feeling which has been favourable to Great Britain in this war".

Wimbourne presented himself well – making it clear that his position of Lord Lieutenant was the weakest of the Executive. He spoke of his tour throughout the country, when he had received the impression of loyalty everywhere and mentioned that the Chief Secretary had always advocated the presence of more troops in Dublin: "Several times in my year of office, he expressed his anxiety for a display of powering the capital". However, he then strongly criticised both Nathan and Birrell for ignoring his good advice – including his insistence that the Castle guard needed to be strengthened. Major Price (see no. 3, with moustache, opposite – who died in a shoot-out in Talbot Street) explained that he performed the additional duties of a country Inspector of the R.I.C. and acted as intermediary between them, the D.M.P., the Military authorities, Dublin Castle and the Under Secretary. He was openly antagonistic to both Birrell and Nathan and said that they were guided by the opinions of outsiders and "went against my opinion

altogether" (He became a 'Companion of the Distinguished Service Order' the following year.

The Commission's report was released at the end of June. It declared, *inter alia*, that 'We consider that the importation of large quantities of arms into Ireland after the lapse of the Arms Act, and the toleration of drilling by large bodies of men first in Ulster, and then in other districts of Ireland, created conditions which rendered possible the recent troubles in Dublin and elsewhere'; The reluctance of the Irish Government to repress by prosecution was largely prompted by the pressure brought to bear by the Irish Parliamentary representatives. 'On the outbreak of [the world] war, all drilling and manoeuvring by unrecognised bodies of men, whether armed or unarmed, should have been strictly prohibited'; that the Irish Government should have forcibly suppressed the Irish Volunteers and the Citizen Army' and that; 'at the risk of a collision early steps should have been taken to arrest and prosecute leaders and organisers of sedition'.

It was outside the scope of their terms of reference 'to enquire how far the policy of the Irish Executive was adopted by the Cabinet'. Their findings were as follows: Chief Secretary Birrell, 'as the administrative head of Your

Majesty's Government in Ireland, is primarily responsible for the situation that was allowed to arise and the outbreak that occurred'. Undersecretary Nathan, although very loyal and devoted to official policies, 'did not sufficiently impress upon the Chief Secretary during the latter's prolonged absences from Dublin the necessity for more active measures to remedy the situation in Ireland, which on December 18th last in a letter to the Chief Secretary he described as "most serious and menacing". No other individual or group was censured. [86]

The rebel prisoners returned from internment in Wales, in 1917, to a heroes' welcome. The new Prime Minister, Lloyd George, appointed the 'uncompromising' Field Marshall Viscount French of Ypres as Lord Lieutenant (1918-21) of (as described it in the latter's letter of acceptance) 'a quasi military government with a soldier in command'. The new Chief Secretary Shortt was made subordinate to French but held a seat at Cabinet. The Prime Minister also appointed a number of moderate Catholics to important administrative and judicial positions in a failed bid to sway the populace. This continued introduction of Irish bureaucratic personnel, which had begun in the 1880s, caused serious friction – 'the Castle,' according to French, 'having become at that stage honeycombed with spies and informers and men who cannot be trusted.' (Most importantly, however, it facilitated the smooth transfer of power to the Irish Free State in 1922, in very troubled times.)

French initiated increasingly severe measures against Sinn Féin, including the arrest of over 1,000 sympathisers, so driving it underground where it proved to be

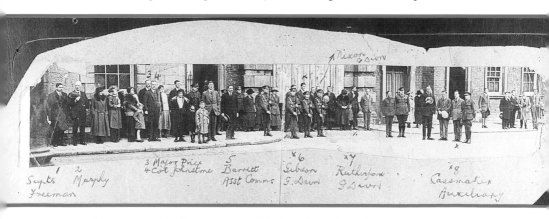

above *Annotated intelligence photograph (and envelope) of British Officers in the Upper Castle Yard (reversed negative) – probably supplied to Michael Collins by Castle staff.*

even more dangerous. In September 1918, two months before the end of the world war, he reported to the Prime Minister that 'harmony had been restored.'

Michael Collins, 'the Big Fellow', who had played a minor role in the rebellion, had become increasingly influential and had risen to prominence as Director of Organisation and Intelligence of the revitalised Volunteer movement, or Irish Republican Army (IRA) as it had become known – which now fought the British forces for control of the country in the slowly escalating, guerrilla-style War of Independence or Anglo-Irish War (1919-21).

He formed a special assassination 'Squad' which narrowly failed an attempt on the life of Viceroy French and systematically killed the Castle's G Division agents. Two of his informants in this Detective Division supplied him with photographs and itineraries. One was Ned Broy, who allowed him access to their files and records. Thomas Markham, a Senior Civil Servant in the Castle, was also an IRA agent and passed him information, as did his cousin, Nancy O'Brien, who had received security clearance and had been put in charge of handling 'the Castle's most secret coded messages' in the G.P.O.'s telecommunication section.

Colonel Ormond Winter,

codenamed 'O', had been sent from London as the new commander of counter-insurgence operations. He was a small, dapper man with a monocle and lived in the Castle, from where he controlled a web of intelligence gatherers and operatives. There was an almost daily series of killings and reprisals. Some IRA men were tortured in the holding cells of the (night-time) Guard House at Exchange Court (adjacent to the Auxiliaries' canteen and G Division) and incriminating information was divulged.

The net was closing on Collins, but he "found out that those fellows we put on the spot were going to put us on the spot, so I got in first". On 'Bloody Sunday' morning 11th November, the 'Squad' assassinated fourteen British Intelligence officers, including some of the infamous 'Cairo Gang'. In retaliation, twelve spectators were killed at a crowded Gaelic football match and Dick McKee and Peadar Clancy (IRA men who were close friends of Collins) and an innocent citizen, Conor McClune, were killed while 'trying to escape' from interrogation in Exchange Court. Their bodies showed clear signs of having being beaten, bayoneted and shot.

According to Dave Nelligan, the other 'Collins spy' in G Division, the effect was devastating as many military personnel and Civil Servants engaged in 'sensitive work'

above The British counter-intelligence Cairo Gang.

were ordered to live in the Castle, where many now sought sanctuary 'like refugees with their personal belongings strapped to their cars. One secret service man shot himself.'

A Castle functionary noted 'the score of prisoners exercising in the Castle yard, who had been rounded up in some raid the night before and housed in the cellblocks and cellars under the State Apartments, before transferral to an internment camp – 'some the type of that under stratum that every revolutionary movement brings to the light; some with the wild and exalted air of the fanatic; a few just quiet looking, good tempered country boys.' He was impressed by General Tudor, head of the reconstituted police force, 'who under the Empire would have made his mark as proconsul of a Roman frontier state'. Tudor's regular departure in his armoured Rolls Royce accompanied by Auxiliaries and Black and Tans (English and Scottish war veterans) bristling with guns, provided all the glamour of war but the bomb-catching meshworks stretched across the gateway, the drapery of barbed wire festooning the guardroom and the ever more pervasive violence depressed morale. [87]

Caroline Woodcock was the wife of a secret-service officer who had been wounded on Bloody Sunday morning. While attending the resultant courts martial in City Hall, she stayed in the Castle which she described as a 'huge rabbit warren where accommodation was at a premium and quite important

above *Liam Neeson as Michael Collins and Alan Stanford as Lord Lieutenant FitzAlan-Howard, salute as the British flag is lowered in Dublin Castle for the last time; from Neil Jordan's Michael Collins.*

people slept two to a room, nay two in a bed sometimes…The army of officials, including the children of police officials, never leave.' Walking around the Upper Yard was the only exercise available, apart from the once a week instruction given by a professor of dancing to officers and their wives in St. Patrick's Hall.

'We never admitted we were at war but all agreed that it was much worse than France – the strain far greater … the only conversation heard is the state of Ireland and the latest rumours.' There was no 'behind the lines' – no relief from the atmosphere of murder and spying. Each time she left the Castle precincts, she was 'followed by eight detectives in Ford cars. As Sinn Féiners were also nearly all clean-shaven and went about in Fords, I never knew if I was being guarded or hunted.'

She once sent a messenger with a telegram to the local post office. While awaiting his return she heard that three unarmed messengers had been shot dead – almost in view of the Castle gates. Paperboys and flower sellers were all part of the Sinn Féin intelligence system. The majority, if not actively involved, supported the insurgents, 'who could fire a shot or throw a bomb, in the absolute certainty that no one will give them away, as they melted into background and the innocent took the brunt of return fire.' [88]

The truce was called on 11th July and the Anglo-Irish Treaty was signed in London on 6th December 1921, by which twenty-six of the thirty-two counties of Ireland – including three from Ulster – formed the Irish Free State (which became a Republic in 1949).

Michael Collins arrived in the Castle on 16th January 1922, to receive the handover on behalf of the new Irish Government. Viceroy FitzAlan-Howard (1921-22, the first Catholic to hold that post since the 1680s) is reported to have grumbled, "You are seven minutes late Mr. Collins," to which he received the reply: "We've been waiting over 700 years, you can have the extra seven minutes."[89] *The Irish Times* wrote: 'Having withstood the attacks of successive generations of rebels, it was quietly handed over yesterday to eight gentlemen in three taxicabs.'

Collins later reflected: 'how could I have expected to see Dublin Castle itself – that dread Bastille of Ireland – formally surrendered into my hands by the Lord Lieutenant, in the brocade hung Council Chamber?' The Dublin playwright Séan O'Casey imagined how FitzAlan-Howard handed over the Castle to him and seemed to be doing it as if in a dream: 'Here's the key to the Throne Room, and this one's the key of St. Patrick's Hall, my good man.'

below The final lowering of the Union Jack by British troops in Queen Victoria (now Collins) Barracks, Cork, on 18th May 1922.

Dublin Castle Today

It is fortunate that the Castle survived the transition to Irish nationhood and wasn't burnt down or blown up like many other monuments of colonialism. However, its political significance much diminished, it suffered neglect and many areas deteriorated and fell into disrepair.

The Supreme Court occupied the

below Séan T. O'Kelly arriving in the Castle *for his inauguration as the second President of Ireland, 1945.*

former Council Chamber, before moving back to the reconstructed Four Courts, that had been reconstructed following the Civil War of 1922-23 (which had been fought between two republican factions over the acceptance of the Anglo-Irish Treaty). Additional government departments and offices were accommodated throughout the complex, including the Department of Industry and Commerce, the Paymaster General, the General Post Office Engineers and Savings Bank, various Revenue Commissioners' Offices and the Children's Court.

Infrequent formal uses included the inauguration of Douglas Hyde as the first President of Ireland, in 1938 and Séan T. O' Kelly as the second, in 1945. The police presence continued throughout the period and, in April 1940, an IRA unit detonated a mine beside a radio base at the old armoury building, seriously injuring five Special Branch officers. Fire extensively damaged the southeast corner of the State Apartments in 1941, which was rebuilt in the 60s along with the adjacent Cross Block, where serious structural problems had first been observed at the beginning of the century.

A four-storey modern office block

Left *Viking antler comb – uncovered during the Castle archaeological excavations.* **below** *View of Castle Hall, Moat Pool and rear of the former 'blind' Gate of Fortitude, by James Horan.*

was constructed in the Lower Yard on the site of the main stables and occupied by the Revenue Commissioners in 1974. George's Hall, which had been built in 1911 as a supper room for the last Royal visit, was adapted for use in conjunction with St. Patrick's Hall for Ireland's first Presidency of the European Union in 1975 – having become a member two years previously.

In the 1980s, funds were allocated to the Office of Public Works (or OPW, which manages the Dublin Castle complex) to implement a large-scale building programme. Archaeological excavations were carried out in advance of these works and uncovered the base of the Powder Tower enclosing a Viking defence bank, the site of medieval Castle Gate, the bases of Corke Tower and the Square Tower and what appears to have been part of the enclosing curtain wall of the early Norman Castle (see descriptions p.15 & ch.5). In addition, almost 100,000 artefacts, ranging from Viking times to the eighteenth century, were recovered from the moat areas. They included bone items (pins, needles, combs and dice), leather scabbards and shoes, knives, arrow and spear heads, coins and tokens, keys and buckles, ceramics, pottery, tiles, glass and bottles from a variety of locations in western Europe.

The eighteenth-century north-east range (Blocks 8-10), which had straddled the infilled moat, was suffering uneven subsidence. Its Upper Yard façade was retained, while the rebuilding above basement level followed along the lines of the original Georgian structures, from which every attempt was made to salvage materials for use in the reconstruction. [90] The adjacent Undercroft was conserved and protected and walkways added for visitor access (see photo p.131).

E.U. Presidency requirements had increased to such a degree that international conference facilities were constructed at the lower-ground floor level between 1987 and 1989, behind the northeast corner façade of the Upper Castle Yard in an area formerly occupied

above The Castle's modern conference facilities. *below* A busy day at the Castle.

above *The Coach House, in the Dubhlinn Gardens.*

by the Castle ditch. The main Conference Hall is partly supported by the excavated base of Corke Tower. The dummy or blind gate of Fortitude (see photo p.124) was opened and a new La Touche bridge gave further access across the new moat pool. Here, the ground level, stone frontage arcade of the former La Touche Bank (which had been constructed in 1735 and encroached on the moat and was taken down in 1945) was re-sited to form the cloistered pool walkway between the Conference Hall and the new Castle Hall.

The top floor of the Bedford Tower building, which had been added in 1820 to provide extra office accommodation and an attic level connection to the Guard House was removed during these renovation works – so restoring the architectural symmetry of the Upper Castle Yard. A modern extension, clad in alternate bands of limestone and granite and incorporating the old Guard House façade, was attached to the rear of

Bedford Tower and together, these serve as the Castle Hall dining and meeting facilities (as shown on left of drawing p.125).

The Dubhlinn Gardens were fitted out as a helicopter-landing pad, with a pattern of six interlocking brick pathways (inspired by Celtic jewellery, see bird's eye view inside front cover) that are distinctive from the air. Artworks by contemporary Irish artists were acquired for the new corner gardens. The traditional connecting footpath which bridges the Back Avenue to Ship Street, was reopened and extended (p.32).

The Lord Lieutenant's Coach House (1833), with castellated frontage to obscure the backs of nearby houses and afford Royal visitors a regal vista, was restored in 1995. Ship Street Barracks, comprising nine terraced houses, were interconnected and 'fitted with a steel-framed construction to compensate for the poor structural condition' [91] and now house Revenue Commissioners' offices

The U-shaped former Army Ordnance Office (1820) was renovated and linked by a glazed concourse to a new, purpose-built, two-storey exhibition area for the relocated Chester Beatty Oriental Library, with its renowned priceless collections – ranging from Babylonian clay tablets (2500 BC) to ancient Irish manuscripts. The eighteenth century Armoury and Treasury Block (p.73) were restored in 1997 and 1992 respectively – the latter with gift shop and restaurant facilities in its barrel-vaulted basement. The more recent Upper Courtyard cobblestone paving provides a reminder of the Castle's military history.

The Dublin Castle site has been occupied over the ages and modified to suit its ever-changing functions. The layers of Irish history reveal themselves throughout the complex – from the Viking defence bank to the State Apartments and from the Chester Beatty Library to the Record Tower's Garda Museum.

The Castle has evolved as Ireland has evolved and has now been fully integrated into Irish society. Today it plays host to leaders of nations, business and industry and history is still being made. It has opened its gates to the citizens of Ireland and peoples of all nations, to experience the unique facilities of Dublin Castle.

Visitor Attractions

The subterranean UNDERCROFT (see photo p.131) features part of the tenth century Viking town defence bank, which is enclosed within the base of the thirteenth century Power Tower (image on p.20 and description on p.32) Also preserved here are the sally port steps cut through the north-eastern curtain wall, the moat archway and part of the medieval town wall.

The Gothic CHAPEL ROYAL (1814, photo p.132) was designed by Francis Johnston (the OPW Architect who was also responsible for Ship Street Gate, the Guard House and the Castle Steps) who 'visibly incorporated it into the eighteenth-century architectural scheme. It is a work of art in its own right.' [92] He employed some of Ireland's premier craftsmen, such as stone and plaster sculptors, Edward and John Smyth; stuccodore, Michael Stapleton; and wood carver, Richard Stewart. The oak galleries and stained glass chancel windows display the coats of arms of the Justiciars, Lord Deputies and Lord Lieutenants – these Viceregal titles succeeded each other over time and were sometimes interchangeable – from the first, Hugh de Lacy (1172) to the last, FitzAlan-Howard

(1921-22), which, remarkably, occupies the final available space.

It functioned as the King's Chapel in Ireland and that of the Viceroy, his household and officials. Lord Lieutenant Whitworth (1813-17) who performed the opening ceremony at Christmas 1814, donated the French stained-glass chancel window. His secluded private gothic passageway to the State Apartments can still be used (see foot of Record Tower in photo p.32). Structural works were carried out in 1989 to stabalise the east end, which was located over an old limestone quarry, [93] as the building was in danger of subsiding into the culverted River Poddle. The restoration project included cleaning of the oak panelling and installation of underfloor heating.

The STATE APARTMENTS were designed in their current form in the 1680's and renovation continued sporadically until c.1761 – with many interiors, including the State corridor, being remodelled since then. The Bedroom suite, Throne Room and St. Patrick's Hall still occupy the site of their medieval equivalents. [94]

The main entrance hall, originally open to the courtyard, leads through a hall of Doric columns to the Imperial double staircase (p.133). The Battleaxe Landing features the Arms of Ireland flanked and complimented by the personal coat of arms of the Presidents of Ireland – each of whom was inaugurated in St Patrick's Hall.

The former STATE BEDROOMS, which consisted of the State bedchamber, dressing rooms, aide de camp's room and study, being structurally unsound, were rebuilt in replica and feature two eighteenth century rococo ceilings. They are now lavishly furnished with paintings, sculptures and furniture from the State collection and the extensive Granard gift, which includes a bust of Philip 11, d'Orleans (see p.134) and a portrait of the Countess of Southampton, c.1640, by Anthony van Dyck.

The c.1830 DRAWING ROOM was largely destroyed by fire in 1941 and was recreated and enlarged to include the Ante Drawing Room (which had been constructed as a Throne Room in 1751). The fireplaces are original. The tall mirrors, pier glasses and consul tables were salvaged and faithfully restored by OPW and the plasterwork was replicated from remnants and photographs.

The THRONE ROOM, which was also known as the Presence Chamber, was first used as a waiting room and was converted during the 1790s to become one of the most important rooms of State. Here, visiting sovereigns received the homage of loyal subjects and incoming Viceroys were ceremonially inaugurated, hosted the Sunday afternoon levées and held their farewell receptions. The lion (representing England) and unicorn (Scotland) canopy may date from that period and the throne was installed for the visit of King George IV in 1821. The splendid, locally manufactured, gilt chandelier and 18th century Gaetano Gandolfi paintings were acquired by OPW in 1839 from sums voted in the annual estimates 'for the gradual improvement and current repairs to the Lord Lieutenant's residences at the Castle and Park'. The ceiling was raised to 'improve the architectural character of the room' in time for the visit of Queen Victoria in 1849 and the crown-shaped mirrors were introduced soon afterwards.

The PORTRAIT (or PICTURE) GALLERY (photo p.136) was formerly the State Dining Room and most of the panelling dates from 1747. It features Venetian glass chandeliers and the portraits of thirteen of the nineteenth-century Viceroys – many of whom have Dublin streets named after them. The Doric columns mark a pre-1767 division into a suite of three rooms.

ST. PATRICK'S HALL is the main public room in Ireland, the largest public space in the Castle and the focal point for important State functions, including the Inaugurations of Irish Presidents. Originally, it was a ballroom with tiered seating around the walls and its present appearance is the result of almost 250 years of changes and improvements. The galleries were erected in the 1760s for musicians at one end and visitors at the other and the fronts were replaced in the 1840s (see Ball p.99 and photo p.137).

The three ceiling paintings are by Vincenzo Waldré (1780s) and depict St. Patrick converting the pagan Irish to Christianity (photo p.8); a baroque-style allegorical scene of King George III seated between Britannia and Hibernia; and King Henry II receiving the submission of the Irish Chieftains in 1172 (photo p.14). Waldré was appointed State Architect, but was later demoted to Inspector of Barracks.

The rectangular mirrors date from a nineteenth century refurbishment and, as in the Drawing Room, match the windows. The banners along the walls are those of the Knights of St. Patrick (see ch.14) and include the Royal standard (second from right p.137) – a symbolic relic from Ireland's colonial past.

above left Oval depicting Medicine with Arts and Sciences, by Bartholomew Cramillon
above right Philip 11, duc d'Orléans (1674-1723). *below* The Drawing Room (see also p.108).

References:

1 Daragh Smyth, *A Guide to Irish Mythology* (Dublin 1988). 2 John Montague, 'The Muse of Amergin' from *The Faber Book of Irish Verse* (London 1974) 3 Ibid – Robert Graves, 'The Alphabet Calendar of Amergin' from *The Faber Book of Irish Verse* (London 1974). 4 Edited by S. J. Connolly, *The Oxford Companion to Irish History* (Oxford 1998). 5 E.E.O'Donnell, *The Annals of Dublin Fair City* (Dublin 1987). 6 Bertil Almgren, *The Viking* (New York 1957). 7 Edmund Curtis, *The Making of a Metropolis* (Dublin 1990), Ed. Howard Clarke. 8 Conleth Manning, *Archaeology Ireland Heritage Guide No. 14* (Dublin 2001). 9 Séan Duffy, *Ireland in the Middle Ages* (Dublin 1997). 10 Ann Thérése Robinson, *A History of Dublin Castle to 1684* (Doctoral Thesis 1994). 11 Ibid. 12 Howard Clarke, *Irish Cities* (Dublin 1995). 13 See Ann Robinson. 14 Bernard Guinan, *A Short History of Medieval Dublin* (Dublin 1997). 15 Peter Somerville-Large, *Dublin, The Fair City* (London 1979). 16 See Ann Robinson.17 Allen Figgis, *Encyclopaedia of Ireland* (Dublin 1968). 18 Richard Stanyhurst, in Hollinshed's *Chronicles' of Irelande* (Dublin 1577). 19 Ibid. 20 Ann Lynch and Conleth Manning, *Dublin Castle – The Archaeological Project from Archaeology Ireland, Volume 4 Number 2* (Dublin 1990). 21 Colm Lennon, *Richard Stanihurst, the Dubliner* (Dublin 1981). 22 Howard Clarke, Sarah Dent & Ruth Johnson, *Dublinia* (Dublin 2002). 23 Ed. Clarke and Refaussé, *Directory of Historic Dublin Guilds* (Dublin 1993). 24 Samuel A. Ossory Fitzpatrick, *Dublin – Historical and Topographical Account* (Dublin1907 and Cork 1977). 25 Assay Office, 350th anniversary booklet. 26 See Ann Robinson. 27 J.W. de Courcy, *The Liffey in Dublin* (Dublin 1996). 28 Ibid. 29 Norman Davies, *The Isles- A History* (England 2000). 30 David Edwards, *History Ireland* Vol. 5 (Dublin 1997). 31 Ibid. 32 See Stanyhurst. 33 Ibid. 34 Robert Kee, *Ireland – A History* (London 1980). 35 From Edmund Spenser's, '*The Faerie Queene*' (New York 1979). 36 Richard Bertleth, *The Twilight Lords* (USA 1978) 37 Patrick J. Corish, *The Irish Martyrs* (Dublin 1989). 38 Garrett Mattingly, *The Defeat of the Armada* (London 1970). 39 See Richard Bertleth. 40 T.P. Kilfeather, *Graveyard of the Spanish Armada* (Dublin 1967). 41 Fiona Griffin, *Extracts from Irish Literature* (Dublin 1992) Translated by Robin Flower. 42 James Carthy, *Ireland 1607–1782* (Dublin 1949). 43 Ed. J.Gardiner & N.Wenborn, *The History Today Companion to British History* (London 1995). 44 See James Carthy. 45 Emily Lawless, 'Clare Coast', from the collection *With the Wild Geese* (Dublin 1912). 46 John Ranelagh, *Ireland: An Illustrated History* (Dublin 1981). 47 Conor Cruise O'Brien, *The Great Melody* (London 1992). 48 See *Oxford Companion to Irish History*. 49 Historic

Manuscripts Commission, *Calendar of the manuscripts of the marquis of Ormonde new series* London, vol. V11. **50** Joseph Brady and Annagret Simms, *Dublin Through Space and Time* (Dublin 2001). **51** Dr. Frederick O'Dwyer, unpublished research on the architectural history of Dublin Castle (Dublin 1990). **52** Ibid. **53** Maurice Craig, *Dublin 1660–1830* (Dublin 1980). **54** Susan Hood, *Royal Roots, Republican Inheritance* (Dublin 2002). **55** *The Irish Times*, 9th July 1907. **56** *The Times* (London) 9th July 1907. **57** Myles Dungan, *The Stealing of the Irish Crown Jewels* (Dublin 2003). **58** John Cafferky & Kevin Hannafin, *Scandal and Betrayal* (Dublin 2002). **59** 'Dublin's Role in 1798' by Tommy Graham, from *The Great Irish Rebellion* of 1798, ed. Cathal Póirtéir (Cork 1998). **60** James A. Culliton, *City Hall – The Irish Heritage Series* (Dublin, 1982). **61** Jonah Barrington, *The Rise and Fall of the Irish Nation* (Dublin 1843). **62** *Requiem for the Croppies*, copyright Faber & Faber.**63** Lawrence W. McBride, *The Greening of Dublin Castle* (USA 1991). **64** Kevin C. Kearns, *Dublin Tenement Life* (Dublin 1994). **65** Ibid. **66** Pat Liddy, *Dublin be Proud* (Dublin, 1987). **67** Richard Barry O'Brien, *Dublin Castle and the Irish People* (Dublin 1912). **68** E. Charles Nelson, *The Cause of the Calamity - Potato blight in Ireland, 1845–1847* (Dublin 1995). **69** 'Ideology and the Famine' by Peter Grey, from *The Great Irish Famine* ed. Cathal Póirtéir (Cork 1995). **70** Ibid. **71** Ibid. **72** Frances Gerard Hutchinson, *Picturesque Dublin* (Dublin 1898). **73** Lady Fingal's Memoirs: *Seventy Years Young* (Dublin 1991) – Courtesy of The Lilliput Press. **74** F.E.R., *Historical Reminiscences* – 1849-1900 (Dublin 1901). **75** See Lady Fingall. **76** See F. E.R. **77** 'Madam', *Heart and Home* (England1892). **78** Maureen Keane, *Ishbel, Lady Aberdeen in Ireland* (Dublin 1999). **79** Ibid. **80** *The Irish Citizen*, 19th April 1912 – reprinted by Rosemary Cullen Owens in *Did your Granny have a Hammer?* (Dublin 1985). **81** Peter Galloway, *The Most Illustrious Order of St. Patrick* (England 1983). **82** Hew Strachan, *The First World War* (London 2003). **83** Leon Ó Broin, *Dublin Castle and the 1916 Rising* (Dublin 1966). **84** 'A first hand account by a V.A.D. nurse', published in *Blackwood's Magazine*, August 1922). **85** *Memoirs of a Young Lieutenant* (Enniskillen 1992) – Compiled by and courtesy of D.S. Carrothers. **86** *The Irish Uprising 1914–21*, (Papers from the British Parliamentary Archive) London 2000. **87** Author and publisher not known: *The Last Days*. **88** Caroline Woodcock, *An Officer's Wife in Ireland* (England 1921) and reprinted as *Experiences of an Officers Wife in Ireland* (Dublin 1994) – Courtesy of Parkgate Publications. **89** Tim Pat Coogan, *Michael Collins* (London 1990). **90** *Building for Government: The Architecture of State Buildings, OPW, Ireland 1900-2000* (Dublin 1999). **91** Ibid. **92** Róisin Kennedy, *Dublin Castle Art* (Dublin 1999). **93** See Dr. Frederick O'Dwyer. **94** See *The Architecture of State Buildings*.

ℐmage Credits

Courtesy of Mark McCall – pages 11 and 75.
Courtesy of O'Brien Press – pages 10/11 and 16/17.
Courtesy of Waterford Corporation – page 13.
Courtesy of OPW Historic Properties – pages 25, 29 and 68.
Courtesy of the National Library – pages 27, 71, 85, 86, 91, 103, 110, 114, 119 and 121.
Courtesy of Mary Murphy – pages 47, 49,50, 53, 65 and 69
Courtesy of the Military Archives – page 108.
Courtesy of the National Gallery – pages 77, and 100.
Courtesy of the Genealogical Office – page 79.
Courtesy of OPW Art Management Office – pages 81, 97 and inside back cover.
Courtesy of the Garda Museum – pages 92.
Courtesy of the National Archives – page 94.
Courtesy of the Gorry Gallery and Brian P. Burns Collection – page 99.
Courtesy of Popperphoto – page 112.
Courtesy of the Marquis of Haddo – page 104.
Courtesy of The Irish Examiner – page 123.
The Illustration on page 3 is based on information from the National Libraries' *Maps of Dublin*, ed. Noel Kissane.

𝒜cknowledgements

I would like to thank the following for their help during production of this book:

Anne Robinson, for use of her doctoral thesis *'A History of Dublin Castle to 1684'*. Dr Frederick O'Dwyer, for information on the architectural history of the Castle. Conleth Manning, for archaeological information on the Castle. Thaddeus Breen for information derived from his research. Also: Peter Pearson, Dermot McElwaine, Bernard Guinan, Comdt. Young (deceased) and Tony Kinsella of the Military Archives, Éamonn MacThomáis (deceased), Delores Gaffney of Kilkenny Castle, Inspector Duffy (ex-Garda Museum), Noel Kissane and David McLoughlin of the National Library. Pat Flaherty provided most of the photographs.

right View of Lower Castle Yard, 1816, by R.Havell & Sons - after T. S. Roberts (and 'dedicated by permission to his Excellency the Right Honourable Charles Earl Whitworth, G.C.B., Lord Lieutenant of Ireland and Grand Master of the Order of St. Patrick'). Palace Street Gate is to right and the Back Avenue, leading to Ship Street Gate in the distance, is to left.